Discover ENGLISH 1

Students' Book

IZABELLA HEARN
AND
JAYNE WILDMAN

Contents

Functions	Skills	Revision
Greetings		
Describing people	Discover Skills: Cool People! Study Skill: Reading	Let's Revise! Pronunciation: /h/
Giving instructions	Discover Culture: Homes **Project**: My Home	Let's Revise! Pronunciation: /θ/ /ð/ Song: *Ghost*
Asking for and giving permission	Discover Skills: Water Wonders Study Skill: Listening	Let's Revise! Pronunciation: /æ/ /ɑː/
Telling the time	Discover Culture: UK Meals **Project**: My Meals	Let's Revise! Pronunciation: /ɪz/ /s/ /z/ Song: *Cha Cha Slide*
Making suggestions	Discover Skills: Holiday Fun! Study Skill: Speaking	Let's Revise! Pronunciation: /w/ /v/
Giving directions	Discover Culture: Spies and Detectives **Project**: A Famous Spy	Let's Revise! Pronunciation: /ŋ/ Song: *I Spy*
Talking about the weather	Discover Skills: Festivals Study Skill: Writing	Let's Revise! Pronunciation: /ɪ/ /iː/
Talking about feelings	Discover Culture: School **Project**: My School	Let's Revise! Pronunciation: /t/ /d/ /ɪd/ Song: *Celebrate*
Ordering events	Discover Skills: Star Report Study Skill: Remembering words	Let's Revise! Pronunciation: /ʊ/ /uː/
Expressing preferences	Discover Culture: Captain Cook **Project**: Explorers	Let's Revise! Pronunciation: /ɪ/ /aɪ/ Song: *You Belong To Me*

Starter A

Hello!

www.DiscoveryWeb/the team

Home | Favourites | The Discovery Web team | Email us | Help

Discovery Web

The Discovery Web Team

- People
- Homes
- Animals
- My Life
- Sport
- Detectives
- Celebrations
- School
- Entertainment
- Adventure

Who are we?

Hi! My name's Monica Lewis. I'm eleven. I'm in Year 6. My favourite colour is red and my favourite thing is my MP3 player.

Hello! I'm Gemma Jackson. I'm eleven and I'm in Year 6. My favourite colour is purple. My favourite thing is an animal, but he isn't purple. He's my dog, Smartie!

My name's Felix Jackson. I'm ten. I'm not in Year 6, I'm in Year 5. My favourite colours are black and yellow. My skateboard is my favourite thing.

1 1.2 **Listen and read. Complete the chart.**

Name	Age	Class	Favourite colour	Favourite thing
Monica		Year 6		
			purple	
Felix	10			skateboard

IN THIS UNIT:

Revision
- *to be*
- favourite things
- possessive adjectives
- countries and nationalities
- *this, that, these, those*

Grammar *to be*

I	**am**	ten.
He She It	**is**	in Year 5.
You We They	**are**	in Year 6.
I She They	**am not** **is not** **are not**	ten. in Year 5. in Year 6.

2 Complete the information about Gemma.

1 I *am* eleven.
2 My favourite thing ______ an animal.
3 I ______ in Year 6.
4 Smartie ______ my dog.
5 He ______ purple.
6 My favourite colours ______ blue and yellow.
7 I ______ in Year 5.

3 Match the words.

1	I am	a	You're
2	We are	b	I'm
3	He is	c	She isn't
4	They are not	d	We're
5	She is not	e	He's
6	You are	f	They're
7	They are	g	He isn't
8	He is not	h	They aren't

Grammar *to be*: questions

Am	I	ten?
Is	he she it	in Year 5?
Are	you we they	in Year 6?
Yes, I **am**. / No, I'**m not**. Yes, she **is**. / No, she **isn't**. Yes, they **are**. / No, they **aren't**.		
What**'s** your name?		

4 1.3 Listen and match.

1	What's your name?	a	No, I'm not.
2	How old are you?	b	My name's Felix.
3	Are you in Year 6?	c	No, it isn't.
4	Is your favourite colour red?	d	I'm ten.

5 Read and answer.

1 Is Felix ten? ***Yes, he is.***
2 Is he in Year 6?
3 Is his favourite colour purple?
4 Is his favourite thing a skateboard?
5 Is your favourite thing an animal?

6 Find two questions. Answer the questions.

Starter B
A New Home

1 🎧 1.4 **Listen and read. True or false?**

1 Ben is from the USA. *true*
2 His new home is in England.
3 His favourite thing is his football shirt.
4 His baseball cap is from Liverpool.

Hi! My name's Ben Grant. My family are from New York City, in the USA, but our new home is in England.

Liverpool is my favourite football team. Their matches are great! My football shirt is English, but my Mets baseball cap is American.

My favourite things are my CD player, my Star Wars watch and my mobile phone. It's a camera too!

Watch Out!

match → matches
city → cities
cap → caps

Discover Words

▶ favourite things

2 **Match the words with the objects in the picture.**

watch *3* football shirt baseball cap CD player mobile phone

3 🎧 1.5 **Write the plurals. Listen and repeat.**

1 mobile phone *mobile phones*
2 family ________
3 shirt ________
4 watch ________
5 camera ________

Grammar possessive adjectives

subject pronouns	possessive adjectives
I	my
you	your
he	his
she	her
it	its
we	our
they	their
I am Ben.	**My** name is Ben.

4 Look at the pictures. Complete the sentences.

1

It's *his* baseball cap.

2

It's ______ mobile phone.

3

We're Lucy and Liam and it's ______ CD player.

4

It's ______ dog.

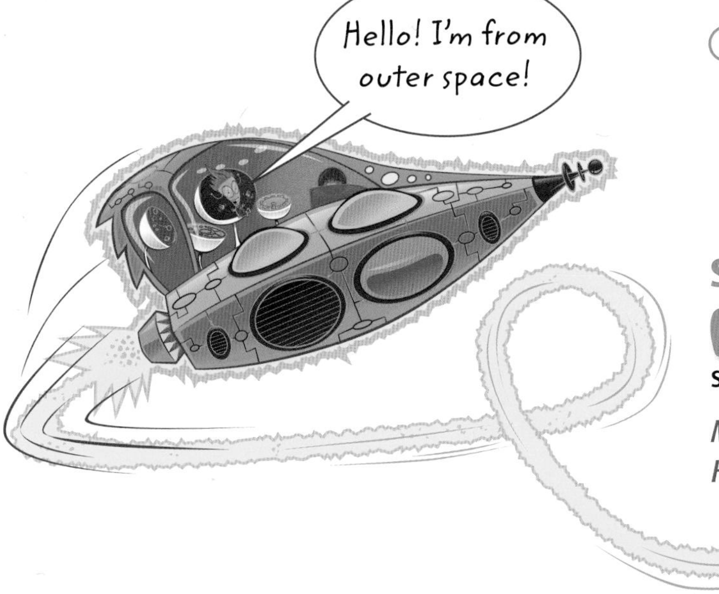

Discover Words

countries

5 1.6 Match the countries and nationalities. Listen, check and repeat.

~~England~~ Portugal Russia Spain Poland Greece Italy Argentina USA Turkey Brazil

Italian American ~~English~~ Russian Portuguese Turkish Greek Brazilian Spanish Argentinian Polish

England English

6 1.7 Complete the sentences. Listen and check.

1

I'm American.
I'm from *the USA*.

2

He's from Argentina.
He's ____________.

3

They're from ____________.
They're Brazilian.

4

She's ____________.
She's from Spain.

5

They're English. They're from ______________.

Speaking

7 Work with a friend. Talk about your favourite stars.

My favourite star is ...
He / She's from ...

Starter C Earth Explorer

1 1.8 **Listen and read. Who is Fiz?**

Grammar *this, that, these, those*

 **this** spaceship	 **that** spaceship
 **these** spaceships	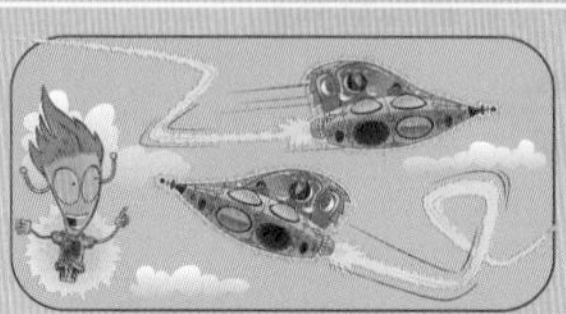 **those** spaceships

2 **Complete. Use *this*, *that*, *these*, *those*.**

1 *This* is my cat.

2 ______ is my CD player.

3 ______ are my football shirts.

4 ______ are my friends.

1 People

Discover Words

appearance

1 1.9 Look and choose. Listen and check.

1 *old / young*
a Lucy is *young*.
b The professor is ___________.

2 *fat / thin*
a Bob is ___________.
b Frozone is ___________.

3 *ugly / good-looking*
a Esmeralda is ___________.
b Quasimodo is ___________.

4 *tall / short*
a Shaggy is___________.
b Daphne is___________.

2 Work with a friend. Describe a character. Use two or three words. Who is it?

tall short fat thin good-looking ugly old young

A *He's tall, fat and good-looking.*
B *He's Bob!*

IN THIS UNIT:
- appearance adjectives
- *have got*
- the family
- possessive *'s*
- describing people

1a A New Friend!

Monica	Hey! That's Ben – the new boy from school.
Felix	Ben?
Monica	Yes, look. He's got a frisbee.
Gemma	Hi, Ben. This is my brother, Felix.
Ben	Hi! Is that your dog, Gemma?
Gemma	Yes. His name's Smartie.
Monica	Hey! He's got my ice cream!
Felix	He's funny!
Monica	Where's the camera?
Felix	Er … I haven't got it.
Ben	Wait. I've got my mobile phone.
	CLICK!
Gemma	That's a great photo.
Felix	Cool! Ha! Ha!
Ben	Look at my funny family photo.
Monica	That's a great photo for Discovery Web.
Ben	What's Discovery Web?
Gemma	Wait and see!

1 1.10 **Listen and read. Who's funny?**

2 **Read the sentences. True or false?**

1 Ben is a new friend. *true*
2 Smartie is a dog.
3 The mobile phone is a camera too.
4 Monica and her family are in the photo.

Talking Tips!

3 1.11 **Listen, repeat and match.**

1 He's funny!
2 Cool!

(A)

(B)

Discover Words

the beach

4 1.12 **Match the words with the pictures. Listen and repeat.**

frisbee *2*   ice cream   beach bag   drink   towel

Grammar *have got / haven't got*

I You We They	**have** **haven't**	**got**	a mobile phone.
He She It	**has** **hasn't**	**got**	a mobile phone.

5 **Look at the photo and complete the sentences.**

1 Ben *has got* a frisbee.
2 Ben and Felix ____________ a towel.
3 Monica ____________ an ice cream.
4 Ben ____________ a beach bag.
5 Gemma and Felix ____________ drinks.
6 Ben ____________ a mobile phone.

6 **Write true sentences!**

Mr Bean I My friends	have got haven't got has got hasn't got	a towel a camera a Mr Bean DVD

Mr Bean has got a camera.

Writing

7 **You and your friends are at the beach. Draw a picture. Then write sentences with *have / has got* and *haven't / hasn't got*.**

I've got a beach bag but I haven't got a towel.
Natalia has got a ... but she hasn't ...
Stefan and Nilgun have got ...

Discover 5 extra words. Go to page 109.

1b A Family Photo

Hi! **Ben** is a new member of the **Discovery Web** team. He's from the **USA**.

Hi everyone!

Discover Words

family

1 1.13 **Listen and repeat. Who are the people in Ben's family photo?**

mum dad brother
sister granny granddad
uncle aunt cousin

2 1.14 **Listen, read and check.**

3 **Read and complete the sentences.**

website brother
~~the USA~~ friends cousin

Ben's family are from [1] *the USA*. He's got two sisters, but he hasn't got a [2] _______. He's got a [3] _______, Danny. Ben's got new [4] _______ in England. They've got a [5] _______, Discovery Web. It's cool!

Who's in your family photo, Ben?

Well, that's my cousin, Danny. He's nine. The tall man is my uncle, Frank. That's my aunt, Sarah. That's my granny and that's my granddad.

Who are the girls? Has Danny got sisters?

No, he hasn't. Those are my sisters.

Have you got a dog?

That's my sister's dog – Bobby.

Thanks Ben and welcome to the Discovery Web team!

Have you got a funny family photo?

E-mail it to *monica@discoveryweb*

Grammar *Have you got …?*

Have	I you we they	**got** a sister?	Yes, I **have**. No, I **haven't**.
Has	he she it	**got** a sister?	Yes, she **has**. No, she **hasn't**.

4 Order the questions.

1 you a dog got Have ?
Have you got a dog?
2 got Has dog Sarah a ?
3 Danny Has brother got a ?
4 a cousin Has got Ben ?
5 granny Have got a they ?
6 Have sister got you a ?
7 website Have got a we ?

Speaking

5 Now work with a partner. Answer the questions in Exercise 4.

A *Have you got a dog?*
B *Yes, I have. / No, I haven't.*

6 1.15 Complete the dialogue. Listen and check.

Charlie and the Chocolate Factory

Ben Hi Felix. [1] ***Have*** you ***got*** a family photo for Discovery Web?
Felix No, I [2] ___________, but I [3] ___________ a photo of a family from my favourite film, *Charlie and the Chocolate Factory*. Look! That's his mum and dad and the old, thin man is his granddad.
Ben [4] ___________ he ___________ a brother or a sister?
Felix No, he [5] ___________.
Ben [6] ___________ he ___________ a granny?
Felix Yes, he [7] ___________. He [8] ___________ two grannies and two granddads.

Fun Zone

7 1.16 Listen and write the words in the grid.

1 *sister* Anna ✓	4	7
2	5	8 *frisbee* Irena ✗
3	6	9

8 Now play *Find Someone Who*. Ask your friends. Tick the boxes.

Maria *Have you got a sister?*
Anna *Yes, I have.*

Maria *Have you got a frisbee?*
Irena *No, I haven't.*

1c Earth Explorer

Fiz is Kit's new friend. He's cool! He's got green hair and orange eyes. He's got a zapper too ...

1

Fiz: Oh no! Where's my zapper?
Kit: I haven't got it.

2

Mum: What's this? Is it Bandit's toy?

3

Bandit: Miiaaaaooowww!

4

Fiz: Oh no! Your mum's got it!
Mum: Is this your toy? Look, here's your English book t
Kit: Great. Bye, Mum!

5

Mum: Bye, Kit!
Bandit: Miaaaaaaaawww!!
Fiz: Ha! Ha!

6

Mouse: Now we are friends!

1 🎧 1.17 **Listen and read.**

Grammar possessive *'s*

Fiz is Kit**'s** new friend.
The zapper isn't Bandit**'s** toy.

2 **Complete the sentences.**

Kit ~~Mum~~ Fiz Bandit

1 It isn't *Mum's* zapper.
2 Fiz is _______ friend.
3 Bandit isn't _______ friend.
4 In picture 6, the mouse is _______ friend.

3 **Break the code! Write the report.**

4 **Act out the Earth Explorer cartoon with your friends.**

Functions: describing people

5 **Complete the chart.**

	Hair	Eyes	Body
Fiz	*short, green*	*orange*	*thin, short*
Kit	*short, blonde*		
Mum	*long …*		

Watch Out!

is + tall, fat, old, good-looking
has got + long hair, blue eyes

6 **Only one sentence is true. Correct the mistakes.**

1 Fiz has got blue eyes.
No, he hasn't. He's got orange eyes.
2 Kit has got short hair.
3 Bandit is thin.
4 Mum and Kit have got brown hair.

7 **Describe someone in your class. Your friend can guess.**

A *She's got long blonde hair.*
She's tall and good-looking.
B *Maria!*

Fun Zone

8 🎧 1.18 **Listen and order the lines. Then listen and repeat.**

☐ It's far away from you.
☐ And orange eyes too.
☐ I'm Fiz from a planet.
1 I've got green hair.

☐ He isn't my friend.
☐ He's ugly and fat.
☐ He's Bandit the cat.
☐ He's got green eyes.

1d DISCOVER SKILLS

Cool People!

Reading

1 Look at the text and choose the correct answer.

Cool people! is:

a about friends.
b about families.
c about famous people.

2 1.19 **Read, listen and check.**

Beyoncé

Try this!

- Look at the text. Where is it from?
  – A postcard?
  – A magazine?

Cool People! Who is your favourite star?

From Hannah in Dublin.
My favourite star is Orlando Bloom! He's tall and very good-looking. He's got brown hair and brown eyes. Orlando is from England. He hasn't got a brother, but he's got a sister. His favourite thing is his dog. His favourite colour is yellow. My favourite colour is yellow too!
Thanks Hannah!

From Sean in London.
Beyoncé is cool! She's tall and thin. She's got long brown hair and brown eyes. Her favourite colour is gold. Beyoncé is American. She's got one sister, but she hasn't got a brother. Her favourite thing is her car.

Orlando Bloom

3 Read the text again. Complete the factfiles.

	Orlando	Beyoncé
Hair	*brown*	
Eyes		
Nationality		
Brothers / sisters		
Favourite colour		
Favourite thing		

4 Complete the sentences.

1 Gold is … *Beyoncé's favourite colour.*
2 Yellow is …
3 Beyoncé's favourite thing is …
4 Orlando's favourite thing is …

Listening

5 1.20 Listen to Monica and Felix. Who is Anna?

6 1.21 Listen again. Circle the correct words.

1 Anna is tall / short.
2 Anna has got brown hair / blonde hair.
3 Her hair is long / short.
4 Anna's eyes are green / blue.
5 She's funny / thin.

7 Look at the photo of LeBron James. Complete the factfile.

Hair	
Eyes	
Nationality	*American*
Brothers / sisters	*no*

LeBron James

8 1.22 Two friends play Ten Questions. Complete their dialogue. Listen and check.

A Well, which star are you?
B It's a game. Guess!
A Are you good-looking?
B Yes, I [1] *am*.
A [2] ____________ you got blonde hair?
B No, I [3] ____________.
A Have you got brown eyes?
B Yes, I [4] ____________.
A Are you short?
B No, I'm [5] ____________.
A [6] ____________ you LeBron James?
B Yes, I am!

Speaking

9 Now imagine you are your favourite star or a star from this lesson. Play Ten Questions and guess the star. Answer *yes* or *no*!

A *Are you tall?*
B *No, I'm not.*
A *Have you got …*

Writing

10 Write about a famous person. Choose your favourite star or write about a star from this lesson.

Beyoncé is my favourite star. She's tall and …

What has got four red eyes and a green body?
I don't know, but there's one in your hair!

1e Let's Revise!

Words

1 Circle the words.

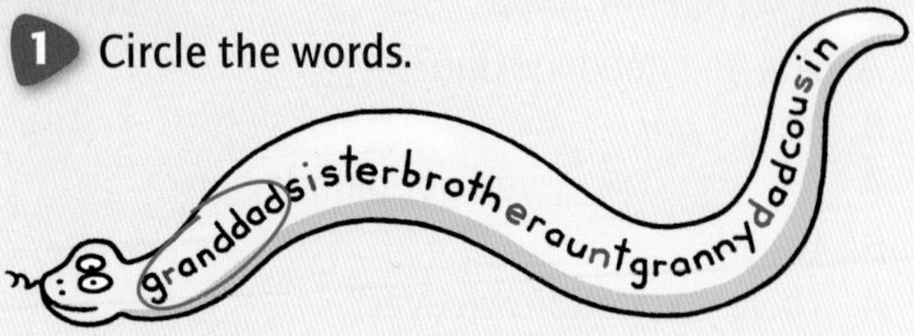

2 Use the red letters in Exercise 1 to find the missing word.

I've got great f_____________.

3 Write the numbers.

towel *1* drink beach bag ice cream frisbee

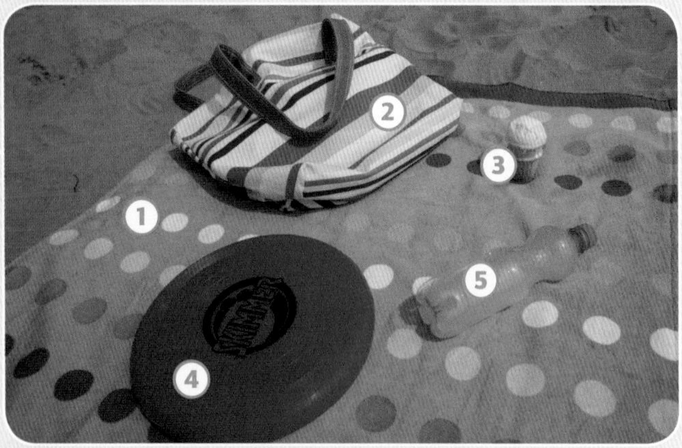

4 Find the opposites.

tall *short*

Grammar

5 Write questions and answers. Use *have got*.

1 Felix / granddad ✓
Has Felix got a granddad? Yes, he has.
2 Monica / cousin ✗
3 Ben / granny ✓
4 Gemma and Felix / aunt ✗

6 Complete the sentences. Use *'s*.

1 Monica is *Gemma's friend*. (friend, Gemma)
2 Smartie is _____________. (dog, Gemma)
3 Gemma is _____________. (sister, Felix)
4 Bandit is _____________. (cat, Kit)

Pronunciation /h/

7 1.23 Listen and repeat.

Henry's **h**orse **h**as got **h**orrible purple **h**air.

Functions

8 Work with a friend. Student A, describe a character from Unit 1. Student B, close your book and guess!

Checklist ✓

- I can use appearance adjectives. ☐
- I can use *have got*. ☐
- I can talk about families. ☐
- I can use possessive *'s*. ☐
- I can describe people. ☐

2 Homes

Our new webpage is about homes. What's your home like?

Discover Words

rooms

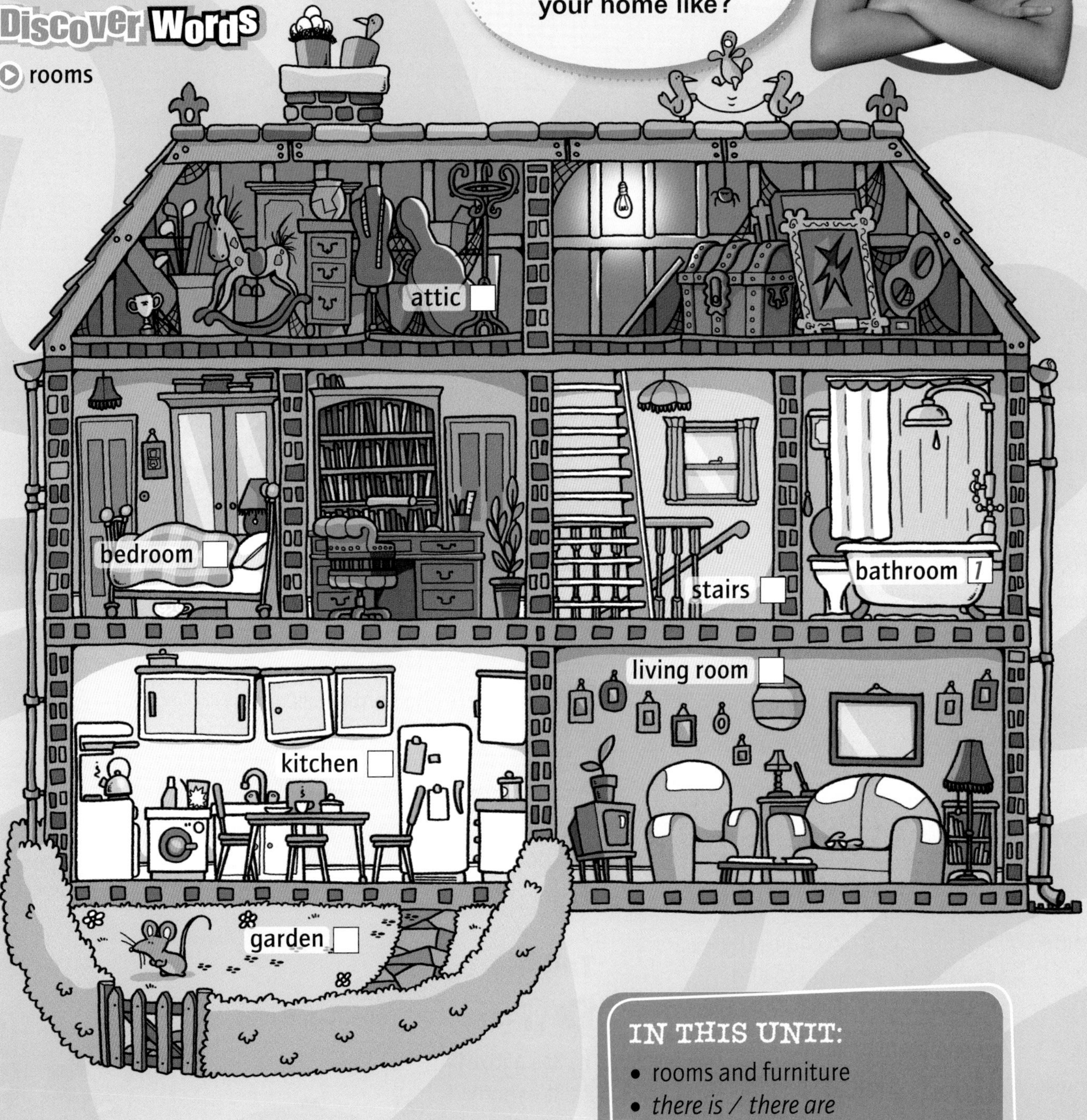

IN THIS UNIT:

- rooms and furniture
- *there is / there are*
- prepositions of place
- imperatives
- giving instructions

1 1.24 Where does the mouse go? Listen and number the rooms.

2 1.25 Listen, check and repeat.

Discover 5 extra words. Go to page 109.

2a It's Spooky!

Gemma Hello… Granddad … Granddad?
Felix Where is he?
CRASH!
Felix Listen! Who's in the attic?
Gemma It's Granddad …
Felix Or a ghost!
Gemma Oh Felix, there aren't any ghosts!
Felix Yes, there are … Wooooooo!

In the attic.

Felix It's spooky!
Gemma Yes, it's very dark. There aren't any windows.
Felix What's in here?
Gemma There are some old chairs, there's a table, there's a bookcase and …
CRASH!
Felix Hey, there's a ghost!
Gemma Oh Felix, it's Granddad's pet cat, Sophie.
Felix Wait! There's a message in the mirror!
Gemma It's a joke, Felix. It's Granddad's joke!
Granddad Felix, Gemma! Where are you?

1 🎧 1.26 **Listen and read. Where are Felix and Gemma?**

2 **Complete the sentences.**

ghost ~~attic~~ table cat

1 The *attic* is dark and spooky.
2 It's got a ______ in it.
3 Has it got a ______?
4 Granddad has got a pet ______.

Talking Tips!

3 🎧 1.27 **Listen, repeat and match.**

1 It's a joke!
2 It's spooky!

(A)

(B)

Discover Words

furniture

4 1.28 **Listen and repeat.**

1 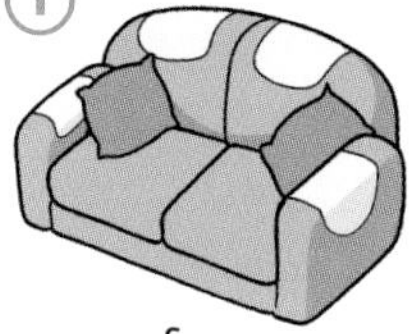
sofa

2 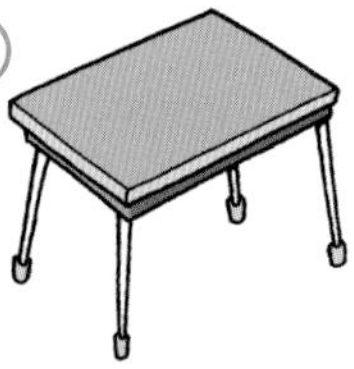
table

3 
mirror

4 
bookcase

5 
cupboard

6 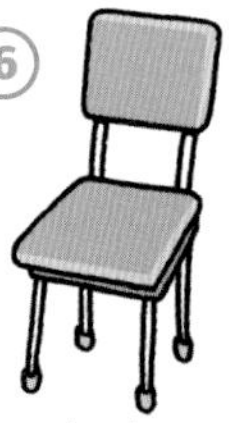
chair

7 
bed

8 
bath

9 
toilet

10 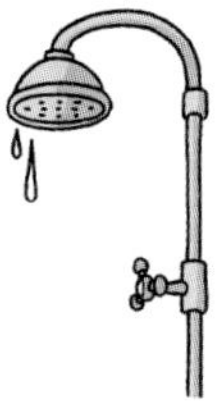
shower

11 
desk

12 
fridge

Grammar *there is / there are*

There is / There's **There isn't**	a table	in the attic.
There are some **There aren't any**	windows	in the attic.
What **is there** in the attic?		

5 **Complete Gemma's diary. Use** ***there is / there isn't / there are / there aren't.***

14th May

I'm at Granddad's house today. My favourite room is the attic. It's Sophie's favourite room too – she's Granddad's cat. The attic is very spooky! 1 <u>There aren't</u> any windows so it's very dark. 2 ___________ some chairs and 3 ___________ a big bookcase. 4 ___________ an old mirror in the attic with a funny message, but 5 ___________ a ghost!

6 **Write sentences about Granddad's house.**

There's a There isn't a
There are some There aren't any

1 TV in the kitchen ✓ *There's a TV in the kitchen.*
2 mirror in the bathroom ✓
3 books in the bedroom ✓
4 shower in the garden ✗
5 ghosts in the attic ✗

Fun Zone

7 **Roll a dice and choose a room. Roll again and choose an object. Then make a sentence about your house.**

1 bedroom	1 ghost
2 living room	2 fridge
3 bathroom	3 shower
4 attic	4 cupboards
5 kitchen	5 desks
6 You choose!	6 toilet

attic / desks *There aren't any desks in my attic.* OR *There isn't an attic.*

2b Fun Homes

Have your family or friends got a FUN HOME?

What's cool about it?
Has it got windows?
Is there a bathroom and a kitchen?
Are there any stairs?

Photos and letters for the Discovery Web, please!

1 1.29 **Read and listen. Match the letters with the photos. There is one extra photo.**

1

A

Hi Monica

Here's a photo for the school webpage. It's my uncle's house in Australia. It's very hot in his town and lots of the houses are underground! My uncle's house is underground, but it isn't dark. There are four windows, but they're very small. There's a living room. It's a kitchen too. There's a TV on the fridge. It's also got a table and some chairs. There's a bathroom next to the living room and one bedroom. There aren't any stairs. It's a really fun house!

Finn

B

Hi Monica

This is a fun home for your webpage. It's my granny's plane house! My granny is from Montana in the USA and her house is an old plane. It's very long. It's got lots of windows so it's very light. The garden is behind the plane. There are stairs from the garden.

There are three bedrooms and there's a kitchen and a living room. There's a sofa and a big TV in the living room. There are lots of cupboards too! There's a new bathroom next to the bedroom. It's got ten windows!

Jenny

Grammar *Is there … / Are there …?*

Is there a bathroom?	Yes, **there is**. No, **there isn't**.
Are there any windows?	Yes, **there are**. No, **there aren't**.

2 Which house, A or B?

1 It's in America. *B*
2 It's got four windows.
3 There aren't any stairs.
4 There's a big television.
5 There's a fridge in the living room.
6 There are lots of cupboards.

3 Write questions.

1 stairs *Are there any stairs?*
2 garden
3 three bedrooms
4 fridge in the living room
5 table in the kitchen
6 television
7 windows
8 cupboards in the living room

2

3

Grammar prepositions of place

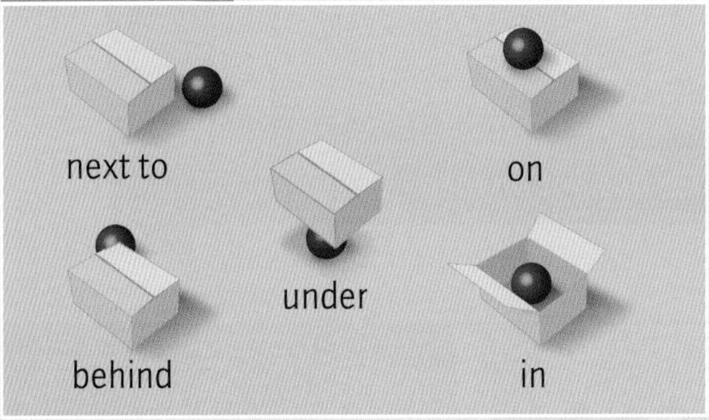

Listening

4 1.30 **Listen to Monica's interview with Alex. What's under the bed in his treehouse?**

5 1.31 **Listen again. Circle the correct words.**

1 Alex's treehouse is (in) / next to the garden.
2 There are some books and games on / under the desk.
3 His skateboard is on / behind the chair.
4 There's a cupboard with some drinks in / on it.
5 There's a bed behind / next to the desk.

Speaking

6 **Choose a fun home. Ask and answer with a friend.**

A *Are there any stairs?*
B *No, there aren't.*
A *Is there a fridge in the living room?*
B *Yes, there is.*
A *Is it the underground house?*
B *Yes, it is.*

Writing

7 **Imagine a treehouse and draw it. Then choose four things. Where are they in your treehouse? Write four sentences.**

bed cupboard TV fridge desk bookcase books skateboard chairs sofa games

There's a sofa next to the door.

2c Earth Explorer

Mindy, Kit, Fiz and Mum have a day at Warwick Castle.

Kit: Mindy is my friend. Don't talk at the castle. You're a secret!
Fiz: Huh! Mindy! And what's a castle?

Mindy: Wow! Are there any ghosts in the castle?
Mum: Wait and see!

Mum: And this is the King's bedroom. Hey! Don't sit down.

Fiz: Ha! Here's your ghost, Mindy!

Mindy: Kit! Look! There *are* ghosts in the castle!
Kit: Oh really … where?
Mindy: There – on the table!

Kit: Don't be silly. It's a mouse!
Mindy: Oh, right. OK.
Kit: Fiz! Stay there and be good!

1 1.32 **Listen and read.**

2 **Answer the questions.**

1 Who is Mindy? *Kit's friend*
2 Is picture 1 Kit's bathroom?
3 Is the castle small?
4 Who is under the helmet?
5 Is there a ghost in the castle?

3 **Help Fiz with his report. Find the sentences.**

REPORT FROM EARTH

Castles|arebigandold.Kit'sfriendissilly.
Castles …

4 **Act out the Earth Explorer cartoon with your friends.**

Grammar imperatives

Positive	Negative
Wait! Be good!	Don't talk! Don't be silly!

What do ghosts eat?
Spookghetti!

Functions: giving instructions

5 1.33 **Match the words with the pictures. Listen, check and repeat.**

Hurry up! *1*   Don't talk!   Be nice!   Don't sit down!
Stay there!   Don't touch!

6 **Now give your partner instructions.**

Fun Zone

7 1.34 **Listen and complete. Then listen and sing.**

~~Open~~   Be   Don't touch   Listen   stay there
Hurry up

There's a ghost in the castle.
Come here and look.
1 *Open* the door.
2 ___________ quick!
3 ___________!

4 ___________ the table.
Don't sit on the chair.
5 ___________ to Mum.
Please 6 ___________.

What's there, Mindy?
It's a very old house.
Is it a ghost?
Or only a mouse?

2d Let's Revise!

Words

1 Circle the rooms.

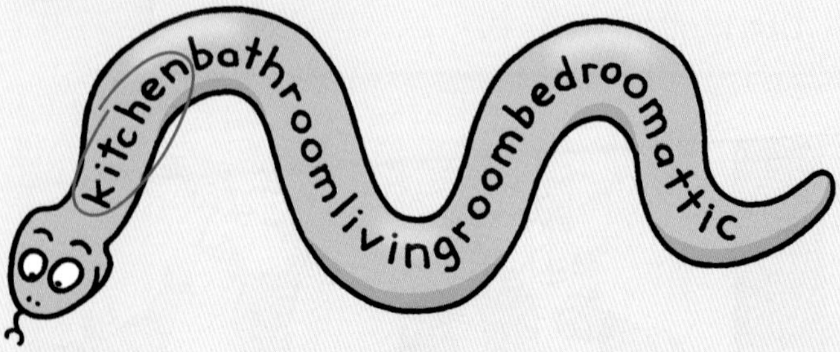

2 Circle the odd one out.

1 table bed garden desk
2 mouse mirror dog cat
3 fridge shower toilet bath
4 books magazines cupboard diary
5 skateboard chair fridge cupboard
6 ball frisbee bike baseball cap

Grammar

3 Complete the sentences about Peggy's room. Use *There is / are* and *There isn't / aren't*.

1 *There aren't* any books on the table.
2 ___________ a drink under the chair.
3 ___________ some balls behind the door.
4 ___________ a cat on the bed.
5 ___________ a frisbee under the bed.
6 ___________ any magazines next to the bag.

4 Write four sentences about Poppy's room. Use *There is / are* and *There isn't / aren't*.

Pronunciation /θ/ /ð/

5 1.35 Listen and repeat.

There are three thin brothers in the bathroom.

Functions

6 Complete the instructions. Use these words.

be ~~sit~~ don't hurry close stay

1 *Sit* down on the blue chair.
2 ______ touch that – it's hot.
3 Granddad's here today – _____ good!
4 ______ the window, please. It's cold in here.
5 ______ there and wait for your mum.
6 ______ up. We've got an English class now.

Consolidation

7 1.36 **Listen and complete the dialogue.**

Felix	Hi, Gemma. Where are you?
Gemma	I'm at 1 *Granddad's* house.
Felix	Oh good. Listen! Are there 2 ________ school books on the table in the living room?
Gemma	No, there 3 ________, but there's a bag 4 ________ the chair.
Felix	A bag! Great! 5 ________ there a green school book in the bag?
Gemma	No, there aren't any books in the bag, or 6 ________ the bag.
Felix	Oh, 7 ________ got an idea! 8 ________ in the kitchen! Are there any books on the 9 ________?
Gemma	No, Felix. There are 10 ________ drinks, but there aren't any books.
Felix	Oh Gemma. Help!
Gemma	Wait! Granddad's in the garden.
Granddad	Hi Gemma! Have you 11 ________ a green school book? There's one 12 ________ the bike.
Gemma	Thanks, Granddad. It's 13 ________ book.

Checklist ✓

- I can describe rooms and furniture.
- I can use *there is / there are*.
- I can use prepositions of place.
- I can use imperatives.
- I can give instructions.

Song

8 1.37 **Complete the song. Use these words.**

walls bed chair ~~hall~~ room door stairs

9 1.38 **Listen, read and sing.**

Ghosts

There's a ghost down in the 1 *hall*
There's a ghoul upon the 2 ______
There's something in the 3 ______
There's a ghost up on the 4 ______
And it's floating through the 5 ______
And there's nothing I can see
And I know that that's the truth
Because now it's onto me

I don't understand it!
Hey!
I don't understand it!
Aaow!

There's a tapping in the floor
There's a creak behind the 6 ______
There's a rocking in the 7 ______
But there's no one sitting there

I don't understand it!
Hey!
I don't understand it!
Hey!

2e Discover Culture

We've got a small flat. There's a living room and a kitchen with a big fridge. There are two bedrooms and there's a bathroom with a shower too. We haven't got an attic or a garden. My favourite room is my bedroom. There's a bed, a desk and a small cupboard for my books. Everything in my bedroom is purple!

My home is a typical English house. It's small but we've got a garden. There are three bedrooms. My bedroom isn't big but it isn't dark. The bathroom isn't light and it's old too. We've got a small kitchen and a living room with a table and a sofa for the family. There isn't an attic.

Reading

1 1.39 Read, listen and complete.

	Bathroom	Bedrooms	Garden	Attic
House			✓	
Flat		2		

Project

My Home

2 Ask and answer the questions with a friend.

1 Is your home old or new?
2 Is there a garden?
3 Are there any stairs?
4 Is there an attic?
5 Are the rooms big or small?
6 Are there two / three bedrooms?
7 Has it got a bath or a shower?
8 Are there any ghosts in your home?

3 Now draw and describe your home.

3 Animals

Discover Words

animals

1 1.40 Match the words with the photos. Listen, check and repeat.

giraffe *1* squirrel bat elephant parrot monkey turtle tiger dolphin shark chameleon

2 Work with a friend. Mime an animal. What is it?

IN THIS UNIT:
- animals
- *can / can't*
- action verbs
- body parts
- asking for and giving permission

3a They're Amazing!

1 1.41 Listen and read. Match the photos with the descriptions.

www.DiscoveryWeb/animals

Look at these amazing animals for Discovery Web. They're amazing!

A Dolphins are cool! They can jump and they can sing. This dolphin's name is Sam. He's amazing because he can paint. His pictures are red and blue and yellow but dolphins can't see colours. They can only see black and white!

2

C Is it a bird? Is it a fish? No, it's Twiggy the squirrel! Twiggy is a grey squirrel from Florida. He can run and climb trees. He can water ski too but he can't swim or fly – bad luck, Twiggy!

1

B This is the Thai Elephant Orchestra. Jabu and her friends are from Asia and they can play music. They can play the drums but they can't play the guitar.

3

2 Read and answer.

1 Which animal is from Asia?
2 Where is Twiggy from?
3 What is the dolphin's name?

Discover Words

action verbs

3 1.42 Match the words with the pictures. Listen, check and repeat.

swim *2* jump run water ski play music
sing paint climb fly dance

Discover 5 extra words. Go to page 109.

Grammar *can / can't*

I You He She It We They	can can't	swim. climb. play music. paint. water ski.

Scrat

4 **Complete the sentences. Use *can* or *can't*.**

1 The elephants in the Thai Elephant Orchestra *can* play music.
2 Sam ______ paint.
3 Jabu ______ play the guitar.
4 Twiggy ______ fly.
5 Dolphins ______ sing.
6 Dolphins ______ see colours.

5 **What about you? True or false?**

1 I can swim.
2 I can't play the guitar.
3 My friend can play the drums.
4 My father can't paint nice pictures.
5 My granny can water ski.

6 **Correct the false sentences.**

My granny can't water ski.

Writing

7 **Read about Lenny. Then write about Scrat.**

Lenny is a shark. He's from the film Shark's Tale. He can swim and sing but he can't jump or climb.

	Jump	Swim	Climb	Sing
Lenny	✗	✓	✗	✓
Scrat	✓	✗	✓	✗

Listening

8 1.43 **Read and choose. Listen and check.**

bat dolphin tiger

1 It can run and climb. It can't fly. What is it? It's a ______!

2 It can swim and jump. It can sing too, but it can't run or climb. It's a ______!

3 It can fly in the dark but it can't jump. It's a ______!

Speaking

9 **Now you play the game. Make question cards and ask your friends!**

It can ...

It can't ...

It's a ...

Lenny

3b Animal Robots

Gemma, Ben, Monica and Felix are at the Animal Robot Exhibition.

Monica Wow! Look at these robot animals. They're really big and they can move!
Gemma We can write about them on Discovery Web.
Ben That giraffe is amazing. Look at its long neck!
Felix Hey! Can you see the chameleon?
Monica Where?
Felix There! It's blue and green. It's next to the giraffe. It's really cool!
Ben What's this?
Gemma It's a bat.
Ben A bat? No way!
Monica Yes, it's got ears, a mouth… and there are its feet.
Ben Where's Felix?
Felix Look! I'm Batman!
Monica Very funny, Felix! Can you fly?
Felix Ouch! Er, no I can't.
Gemma Come on Felix, let's go.

1 1.44 **Listen and read. True or false?**

1 The children are at a zoo. *false*
2 The robots can't move.
3 The chameleon is different colours.
4 The bat has got a long neck.
5 Felix can fly.

Talking Tips!

2 1.45 **Listen, repeat and match.**

1 No way!
2 Come on.

A

B

Discover Words

body parts

3 1.46 **Listen and repeat. Point to the body parts of Felix and the robot dog.**

head eye ear nose mouth tooth
neck hand finger leg foot arm hair

Grammar *Can you…?*

Can	I you he she it we they	swim?
Yes, we **can**. / No, we **can't**.		
What **can** they do?		

Listening

4 **Order the questions about Aibo, the robot dog.**

1 can What do he ? *What can he do?*
2 Can jump Aibo ?
3 What say can he ?
4 sing he Can ?

5 1.47 **Match the questions with these answers. Listen and check.**

a Yes, he can.
b No, he can't.
c He can say *hello* and *goodbye*. *3*
d He can walk and run.

Speaking

6 **Practise with a friend. Use the action verbs on page 30.**

A *Can you swim?*
B *Yes, I can. / No, I can't.*

Watch Out!

one tooth → two teeth
one foot → two feet

Fun Zone

7 1.48 **Listen and complete the rap. Use these words.**

feet eyes mouth teeth hands ~~legs~~

Have you got long [1] *legs*?
Can you stand and walk?
Have you got a big [2] _______?
Can you sing and talk?

Have you got white [3] _______?
Can you eat, eat, eat?
Can you jump and run home
On your two big [4] _______?

Have you got two [5] _______?
Can you see and cry?
Have you got two [6] _______?
Can you wave goodbye?

8 1.49 **Now listen again and say the rap.**

3c Earth Explorer

Kit and Fiz are at the zoo.

1

Fiz: Wow! This is a cool place.
Kit: Can I take photos?
Girl: Yes, you can. But you can't touch the animals.

2

Kit: They're monkeys. They can jump and climb.
Fiz: Can I touch them?
Kit: No, you can't!
Parrot 1: No, you can't!

3

Fiz: Hello. Can you talk?
Parrot 1: Yes, we can. We can fly too.
Parrot 2: We're very clever and very beautiful.

4

Fiz: Oh no, it's Bandit's big brother!
Parrot 1: It's a tiger. You can touch it.
Parrot 2: Yes, you can. It's very slow.

5

Tiger: Roooaaar!
Fiz: Aaarrggh! It isn't slow, it's fast!

6

Kit: Fiz! You can't touch the animals in the zoo. They're dangerous.
Bandit: … and I'm dangerous too, Fiz. Grrr!

1 1.50 Listen and read.

2 Read the sentences. True or false?

1 There are animals at the zoo. *true*
2 Fiz has got a camera.
3 You can take photos at the zoo.
4 You can touch the animals.
5 The parrots can't talk.
6 The tiger is Fiz's friend.

Discover Words

adjectives

3 1.51 Match the words to the pictures. Listen, check and repeat.

beautiful fast ~~dangerous~~ slow clever

4 Which animal at the zoo – monkey, parrot or tiger:

1 is clever? *monkey, parrot*
2 can climb?
3 is fast?
4 is dangerous?
5 can fly?

5 Break the code! Write the report.

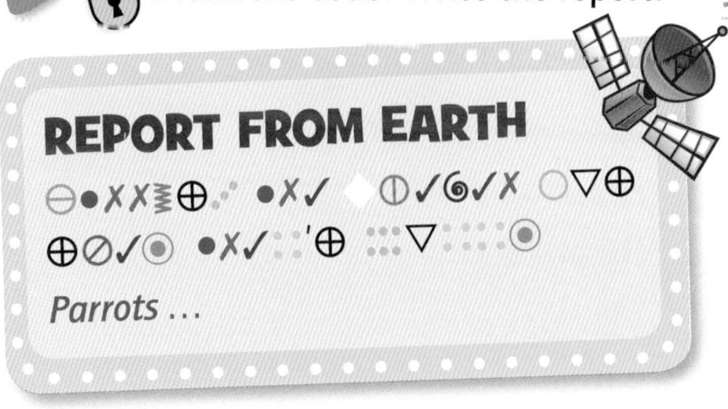

6 Act out the Earth Explorer cartoon with your friends.

Functions: asking for permission

7 1.52 Listen and repeat.

A Can I touch the tiger?
B No, you can't!

A Can I sit down here?
B Yes, you can.

A Can we take a photo?
B Of course you can.

8 Ask and answer with a partner.

✓ Yes, you can.
✓✓ Of course you can.
✗ No, you can't.

1 have a drink ✓✓
Can I have a drink?
Of course you can.
2 paint a picture ✓✓
3 touch the dog ✗
4 take my camera ✓
5 open the window ✗
6 eat these biscuits? ✓
7 sing a song ✓✓

What key can open a banana? A monkey!

3d DISCOVER SKILLS

Water Wonders

Reading

1 Look at the photo. What animal is it?

2 1.53 Read, listen and check your answer.

Dear Alice,

I'm in Lisbon today with my cousins. Lisbon is great! There's an aquarium here. It's very big and there are sharks and turtles. White sharks are amazing! They're big and very beautiful and they can swim very fast. They're dangerous too – they've got lots of teeth!

My favourite animals are turtles. Look at the turtle on the postcard. I've got a pet turtle from Australia and its name is Oliver. Turtles have got long necks and big mouths. They haven't got teeth, so they aren't dangerous. They're very ugly but I think they're great!

Have you got a pet? Write soon!

Best wishes,

Maria

Ormskirk
Lancashire
ENGLAND
UK

3 Read and answer.

1 Where is Maria today? *She's in Lisbon.*
2 What can you see there?
3 Why are white sharks dangerous?
4 What pet has Maria got?
5 Where is Oliver from?
6 Is Oliver beautiful?

Sandtiger shark

Listening

4 1.54 Look at the photo of Gina. Listen and circle the correct answers.

1 Gina is
   a in the Dolphin Park.
   b at home.

2 She is with
   a a guide.
   b a friend.

3 Her favourite animal is
   a a turtle.
   b a dolphin.

4 Dolphins are
   a beautiful.
   b dangerous.

5 There are sandtiger sharks in
   a Australia.
   b England.

Try this!

- Before you listen: look at the pictures. They can give you clues.

5 1.55 Listen again. Complete the factfile about the sandtiger shark.

It's from	
It has got	
It can	

Speaking

6 Work with a friend. Imagine an animal. Your friend asks five questions. Can they guess the animal?

Can it sing?
Is it from Australia?
Is it dangerous?
Has it got big ears?
Is it fast?

Writing

7 Describe your favourite animal. It can be in a zoo or an aquarium, or it can be your pet.

My favourite animal is a ...
It's from ...
It's got ...
It can ...
It's very ...

Gina

3e Let's Revise!

Words

1 Match red and blue letters to make words.

Animals		Action verbs	
squir	affe	ju	n
dol	ger	ru	imb
monk	phin	dan	ce
gir	rel	si	ski
eleph	ark	pai	mp
sh	ey	water	nt
ti	ant	cl	ng

squirrel *jump*

2 Write four true sentences about animals.

fast slow dangerous beautiful clever

Tigers are fast.

3 Label the animal.

~~head~~ eye ear nose mouth hand finger leg foot toe

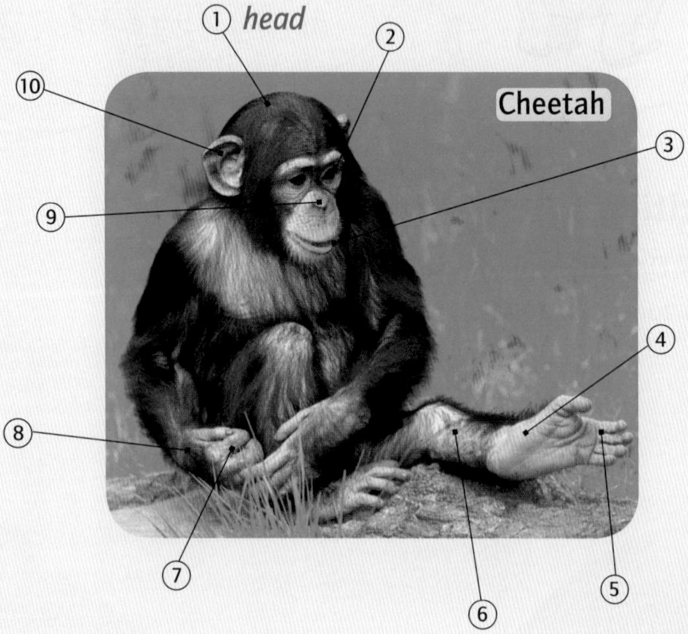

Grammar

4 Complete the sentences. Use *can* and *can't*.

Cheetah is a film star. He's famous and he's very clever. Cheetah [1] *can* do lots of things. He [2] ______ climb trees, he [3] ______ jump and he [4] ______ act. But he [5] ______ fly, he [6] ______ swim and he [7] ______ water ski!

Pronunciation /æ/ /ɑː/

5 1.56 Listen and repeat.

Can bats dance in the bath?
No, they can't.

Functions

6 Order the questions. Match them with the answers.

1 swim with Can I it ?

____

2 Can we it play with ?

____

3 Can see I it ?

____

a Yes, of course you can.
b Yes, look.
c No, it's dangerous.

Checklist ✓

I can name different animals.
I can use *can / can't*.
I can use action verbs.
I can label body parts.
I can ask for and give permission.

4 My Life

Hello!
Our new webpage is about our daily routines. Oh no! I'm late for school!

Discover Words

routines

1 2.2 Listen. Order the pictures.

A walk to school ☐

B watch TV ☐

C have dinner ☐

D meet friends ☐

E study ☐

F finish school ☐

G go to bed ☐

H get up 1

2 2.3 Listen, check and repeat.

3 Is your day the same or different?

IN THIS UNIT:

- routine verbs
- present simple
- transport
- telling the time

4a Daily Routines

1 2.4 Listen and read.

2 2.5 Read and listen. Match Felix's activities to the times.

1 finish school *B*
2 have breakfast
3 get up
4 go to bed
5 watch TV

Talking Tips!

3 2.6 **Listen, repeat and match.**

1 That's disgusting!
2 Go away!

Grammar present simple: affirmative

I You We They	**get up** **watch** TV **study** **have** breakfast	at seven o'clock.
He She It	get**s** up watch**es** TV stud**ies** **has** breakfast	

4 **Circle the correct words.**

1 Ben get up / (gets up) at seven o'clock.
2 His sister watch / watches TV at home.
3 They finish / finishes school at four o'clock.
4 Ben meet / meets his friends at three o'clock.
5 He study / studies then he goes to bed.

Watch Out!

have / eat: breakfast, lunch, dinner, cereal, chips

5 2.7 **Listen and complete.**

Monica [1] *gets up* at seven o'clock. She [2] _______ breakfast with her brother – they [3] _______ cereal. At eight o'clock, Monica [4] _______ to school with her friends. She [5] _______ dinner at six o'clock, then she [6] _______ TV. At nine o'clock, she [7] _______ to bed.

Speaking

6 **Work with a friend. Mime an action and draw a time. Your friend can guess.**

You have breakfast at eight o'clock!

Fun Zone

7 2.8 **Listen and complete. Then listen and repeat.**

Bill gets up and plays the [1] *drums*.
At one o'clock or two.

He has his dinner on his [2] _____.
And watches TV, too.

He studies in the shower or [3] _____.
And finishes at ten.

He says goodnight to
Mum and [4] _____.
And goes to bed again.

Discover 5 extra words. Go to page 109.

4b To School

Discover Words

transport

1 2.9 Match the words with the photos. Listen, check and repeat.

motorbike *1*   bike   plane   car
boat   bus   train

2 2.10 Now listen and match the sounds to the transport.

1 *car*
2 ________
3 ________
4 ________
5 ________
6 ________
7 ________

3 2.11 Read and listen. Match the children to the transport.

1 James — c
2 Amit
3 Dakota
4 Kim

a motorbike
b boat
c bus
d bike

Everyone gets up and goes to school but lots of people don't walk.

Read about these children.

Hi! My name's James and I'm from London. I go to school by bus. It's very slow, but my friends go on the bus too so it's good fun.

Hello, I'm Amit and I'm from India. On school days I get up at six o'clock. I meet my friend Samir and we go to school by bike.

Hello! My name's Dakota and I'm from Alaska. I don't walk to school and I don't go by car. We haven't got a car but we've got a boat and a small plane. My school is next to a big lake so I go to school by boat.

Hi, I'm Kim and I'm from Vietnam. On Mondays I walk to school with my friends, but on Tuesdays I go to school with my big sister. She doesn't walk. She goes on her motorbike and I sit behind!

Grammar present simple: negative

I You We They	**don't**	**go** to school by bus.
He She It	**doesn't**	**go** to school by bus.

4 **Circle the correct words.**

1 James goes / (doesn't go) to school by train.
2 Amit gets up / doesn't get up at 7 o'clock.
3 He goes / doesn't go to school by bike.
4 Dakota lives / doesn't live in Alaska.
5 She goes / doesn't go to school by car.
6 Kim walks / doesn't walk to school with her sister.
7 She meets / doesn't meet her friends on Monday.

Watch Out!

by: bike, motorbike, car, boat, bus, plane, train.
on: foot

Listening

5 2.12 **Listen and tick the boxes.**

	Monica	Ben (in the USA)
walks to school	✓	
goes to school by bus		
listens to music		
finishes homework		
talks to friends		
sings		
reads a book		

6 **Write true sentences.**

1 Monica *doesn't go* (go) to school by bus.
2 Ben and his friends ______ (walk) to school.
3 Monica _____ (listen) to music.
4 Ben and his friends ______ (sing).
5 Monica ______ (read) a book.
6 Ben ______ (finish) his homework on the bus.

Writing

7 **What do you do when you go to school? Tick the list in Exercise 5. Compare with a friend. Write sentences.**

I go by bus but Paola doesn't go by bus. She goes by car. I talk to friends and Paola talks to friends too.

4c Earth Explorer

1 2.13 **Listen and read.**

Grammar present simple: questions

Do	I you we they	**get up** late?
Yes, we **do**. / No, we **don't**.		
Does	he she it	**get up** late?
Yes, he **does**. / No, he **doesn't**.		
What time **do** you **get up**?		

2 **Complete the questions with *do* or *does*. Match the questions with the answers (a–d).**

1 *Do* they live in houses on Fiz's planet?
2 ___ Fiz start work at nine o'clock?
3 ___ Fiz have bats' legs for lunch?
4 ___ Fiz's friends sleep in bags?

a No, he doesn't.
b Yes, he does.
c No, they don't.
d Yes, they do.

3 **Order the questions. Write the answers.**

1 Fiz / by bus / Does / go to work ?
Does Fiz go to work by bus?
No, he doesn't. He goes to work by spaceboard.
2 Fiz / start work / Does / at 72 o'clock ?
3 go to bed late / Fiz / Does ?
4 Where / live / Fiz and his family / do ?
5 What / Fiz's friends / do / eat / for lunch ?
6 sleep / Fiz / Does / in a bed ?

4 **Help Fiz with his report. Find the sentences.**

REPORT FROM EARTH

People|heredon'tliveunderground.
Theydon'teatbats'legs.
People …

5 **Act out the Earth Explorer cartoon with your friends.**

Discover Words

time

6 2.14 **Match the words and the times. Listen, check and repeat.**

1 It's seven o'clock. *A*
2 It's quarter past three.
3 It's half past eight.
4 It's five to twelve.
5 It's ten to nine.
6 It's twenty-five to six.

Functions: telling the time

7 2.15 **Ask and answer. Listen and check.**

A *What time is it?*
B *It's ten past nine.*

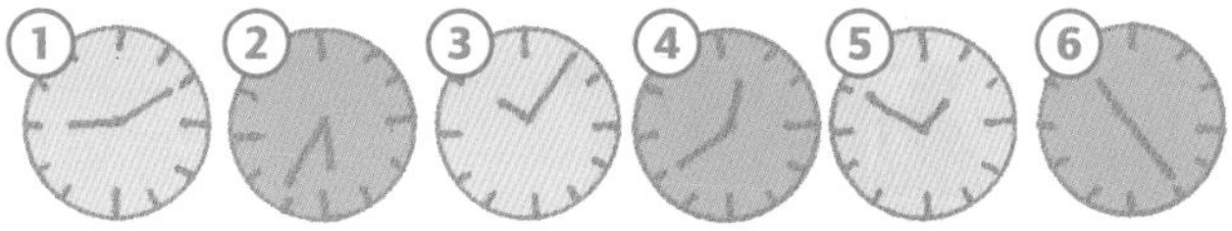

8 **Work with a friend. Talk about your day.**

I have breakfast at half past seven.
I start school at …

4d Let's Revise!

Words

1 Match the words.

1 *finish school*
2 ________
3 ________
4 ________
5 ________
6 ________

get, have, watch, ~~finish~~, meet, go

up, TV, breakfast, to bed, friends, ~~school~~

2 Write the names of the pictures into the grid. The blue column spells out what they are.

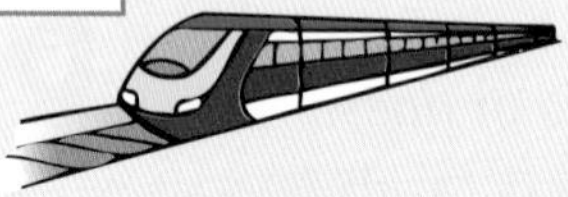

		1 T						
2								
		N						
3								
		4						
	5							
6		T						

Grammar

3 2.16 Complete. Use the verbs in brackets. Listen and check.

Vera Vampire [1] ***doesn't get up*** (not get up) in the morning, she gets up late. She has breakfast at half past nine but she [2] ________ (not eat) cereal! She [3] ________ (meet) her friends at quarter to eleven. They go to vampire school. They [4] ________ (not study) English, they study flying! School [5] ________ (finish) at three o'clock but she [6] ______ (not go) home. Vera [7] ________ (watch) films with her friends. They like films about Dracula. Vera [8] ________ (go) to bed at five o'clock.

4 Order the questions.

1 Vera / Does / early / get up / ?
Does Vera get up early?
2 she / cereal / Does / eat / ?
3 English / they / Do / study / ?
4 Do / they / films / watch / ?
5 Vera / Does / at four o'clock / go to bed / ?

5 Work with a friend. Ask and answer the questions.

A *Does Vera get up early?*
B *No, she doesn't. She gets up in the evening.*

Pronunciation /ɪz/ /s/ /z/

6 2.17 Listen and repeat.

She write**s**, he phone**s**, he come**s** to the show. She danc**es**, he watch**es**, she finish**es**, they go.

Functions

7 Write the times. Practise saying them with a friend.

1 *It's quarter to eight.*

2

3

4

Consolidation

8 2.18 Listen and complete the dialogue.

It's Saturday.
Ben and Felix are at the skate park.

Ben This place is great! What time [1] *does* it open?

Felix It [2] ______ at quarter to eight. I come here with my friends, when we [3] ______ school.

Ben [4] ______ you come here every day?

Felix No. We [5] ______ come here [6] ______ Mondays. It [7] ______ open that day. Look! I [8] ______ jump!

Ben Felix, that's dangerous!

Felix Aaarghh! Ow!

Ben Are you OK? [9] ______ you walk?

Felix Yes, I [10] ______ but I [11] ______ move my arm.

Ben Oh no!

Checklist

I can use routine verbs.

I can use the present simple.

I can describe forms of transport.

I can tell the time.

Song

9 Match the actions with the pictures.

stomp *5*   hop   slide to the right
slide to the left   hands on your knees
crisscross

10 2.19 Listen to the song and number the actions. Listen again and do the actions.

hop 1

Cha Cha Slide

Now it's time to get funky
To the right now, to the left
Take it back now ya'll
1 hop this time, 1 hop this time
Right foot 2 stomps, left foot 2 stomps
Slide to the left, slide to the right
Crisscross, crisscross
Cha Cha real smooth
Let's go to work

Turn it down
To the left, take it back now ya'll
2 hops 2 hops, 2 hops 2 hops
Right foot 2 stomps, left foot 2 stomps
Hands on your knees, hands on your knees
Get funky with it, aahhhh yaaaa.

4e Discover Culture

Reading

1 2.20 Read and listen. Match the food to the times.

UK Meals

Hi, I'm Anna! I'm from Manchester. I get up at seven o'clock and breakfast is at half past seven. I don't like cereal but I eat toast and I have a drink.

Lunch is at half past twelve. I have lunch at school. The food there is OK, but it isn't great. I have sandwiches but my friend Saskia has fish and chips. Chips are her favourite food!

School finishes at quarter past four. I eat an apple when I walk home. My friends eat sweets!

Dinner is at six o'clock and I eat it at the table with my family. We don't watch TV – we talk about our day at school. We eat lots of different food but pizza is my favourite.

2 Anna's friends eat these but Anna doesn't. What are they? Find two answers from the text.

Project

My Meals

3 Answer the questions with a friend.

1 What time do you have breakfast? lunch? dinner?
2 What do you eat and drink at the meals?
3 Do you eat at school or at home?
4 Do you eat with your family or friends?
5 What's your favourite food?

4 Describe and draw your meals.

5 Sport

Hi!
Our new webpage is about sport –
I love sport!

Discover Words

sports

1 2.21 Match the words with the pictures. Listen, check and repeat.

football *1* swimming tennis windsurfing basketball
cycling horse riding volleyball golf sailing

2 Read the clues. Guess the sport.

(1)
I don't play with a ball.
It's a water sport.
I do it on Wednesday after school.
It's great!
It's ___________.

(2)
It isn't a water sport.
I play with a ball.
I play it on Monday.
It's fun!
It's ___________.

3 What about you? Work with a friend.

It's a water sport …

IN THIS UNIT:

- sports
- question words
- *like* + *-ing*
- seasons and time of day
- object pronouns
- making suggestions

5a Sports Heroes

1 2.22 **Listen and read. What is Gisela's favourite sport?**

2 **True or false?**

1 Gisela is twelve. *false*
2 She is a world champion.
3 She is from Spain.
4 She doesn't train every day.
5 She doesn't go to school.
6 She has fun with her friends.

Discover Words

seasons and times of day

3 2.23 **Match the words and the pictures. Listen, check and repeat.**

winter *4* morning autumn
evening spring night
summer afternoon

Hi! Meet our sports hero!

Who is she?
Her name is Gisela Pulido. She's eleven years old. She's the world kitesurfing champion.

Where is she from?
She's from Spain.

Where does she live?
She lives in Gerona, near the beach.

What sports does she like?
Kitesurfing is her favourite sport but she likes swimming, sailing, windsurfing and other summer sports too. She cycles to school every day in spring and summer.

When does she train?
She trains in the afternoon. Her dad is her teacher.

Does she train every day?
Yes, she does. Gisela and her dad train in the afternoon for an hour. Then Gisela does her homework.

What does she do at the weekend?
Gisela has fun with her friends. In summer, she goes on holiday with her family.

4 2.24 **Complete the table. Listen and check.**

~~the evening~~ half past nine winter Friday the morning
Wednesday four o'clock spring the weekend

in	on	at
the evening		

5 **Write true sentences.**

1 I go swimming *in summer.*
2 We do sports ___________.
3 I do my homework ___________.
4 I have fun with my friends ___________.
5 We go on holiday ___________.

Grammar question words

Who is she?	Gisela
What's her favourite sport?	Kitesurfing
Where does she live?	In Spain
When do they go on holiday?	In summer

6 **Complete the sentences.**

1 *Who* is he?	He's Cristiano Ronaldo.
2 ______ has he got?	He's got a football.
3 ______ is he from?	He's from Portugal.
4 ______ does he train?	He trains in the morning.

7 **Write questions about Marat Safin and his sister, Dinara. Answer the questions.**

Name: Marat Safin
From: Russia
Lives: Monaco
Sport: tennis
Trains: in the morning
Likes: football, films, animals

Name: Dinara Safina
From: Russia
Lives: Russia
Sport: tennis
Trains: in the afternoon
Likes: football, music, books

1 who / they ?
Who are they? They are Marat and Dinara.
2 where / they from ?
3 where / Marat / live ?
4 what / sport / they / play ?
5 when / Dinara / train ?
6 what other sport / they / like ?

Fun Zone

8 **Imagine you are a sports star. Work with a friend. Ask and answer about your sports stars. Look at Exercise 7 to help you.**

Who are you? I'm …
Where do you live? I live in …

9 **Complete the factfile about your friend's sports star.**

Name:
From:
Lives:
Sport:
Trains:

5b Saturday

Discover Words

go and *play*

1 2.25 **Write the words in the correct column. Listen, check and repeat.**

volleyball ~~sailing~~ swimming basketball
golf horse riding tennis windsurfing football

we go	we play
sailing	

2 2.26 **Listen and read. Who does lots of things at the weekend?**

3 Answer the questions.

1 When does Gemma finish her dance class?
at 12 o'clock
2 When does she go horse riding?
3 Does she like the teacher at her dance class?
4 Does Gemma write Discovery Web at the weekend?
5 Does Gemma play football on Sunday?

It's Saturday morning. Ben is at Gemma and Felix's house.

Gemma Bye, you two. It's time for my dance class.
Ben What time do you finish?
Gemma At 12 o'clock, but I go horse riding in the afternoon.
Ben Gemma, you don't stop!
Gemma Well, I like dancing. I've got a great teacher. I love horse riding, too.
Felix She's crazy, Ben. On Saturdays she goes dancing and swimming and running and on Sundays she plays tennis and football and volleyball and golf… and writes for Discovery Web, of course!
Gemma Stop it, Felix! I don't like playing football and I hate running and … I'm late. Bye!

Discover 5 extra words. Go to page 109.

Talking Tips!

4 2.27 **Listen, repeat and match.**

1 Stop it!
2 She's crazy!

Grammar *like + -ing*

I You We They	**like / love** **hate / don't like**	**swimming.**
He She It	**likes / loves** **hates / doesn't like**	**swimming.**
Do you **like dancing**? Yes, I do. Does he **like dancing**? No, he doesn't .		
What do you **like doing** at the weekend?		

5 Order the sentences.

1 loves Gemma dancing . *Gemma loves dancing.*
2 like doesn't She football playing .
3 Gemma Does running like ?
4 Ben doing at the weekend What does like ?
5 likes playing He basketball .

6 Write true sentences about you.

1 ☺ I love …
2 ☺ I like …
3 ☹ I hate …

Listening

7 2.28 **Listen to Ben and Monica. Match the questions and answers.**

1 Do you like living here?
2 Do you like walking to school in winter?
3 Do you like watching football on TV?
4 Do you like swimming?

a No, I hate it.
b No, I don't.
c Yes, I do.
d Yes, I love it.

Speaking

8 Complete the table with your own questions. Then ask and answer in groups of four.

✓✓ Yes, I love it. ✗ No, I don't.
✓ Yes, I do. ✗✗ No, I hate it.

Do you like:	Friend 1	Friend 2	Friend 3
running?	✓		
playing tennis?			
painting?			
dancing?			
__________?			
__________?			

Writing

9 Write about your friends.

Ayse and Hasad like running but Olga hates it.

How do vampires play baseball?
With a baseball bat!

5c Earth Explorer

1

2

3

4

5

6

1 2.29 **Listen and read.**

2 **Answer the questions.**

1 What time does the match start? *2 p.m.*
2 Who does Mindy like?
3 Does Becker score a goal?
4 Does Kit like Kingsley or Troy?

3 **Break the code! Write the report.**

REPORT FROM EARTH

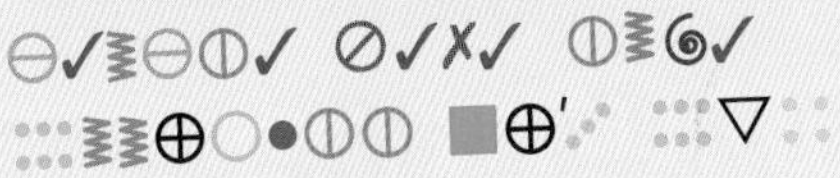

People …

4 **Act out the Earth Explorer cartoon with your friends.**

Grammar object pronouns

subject pronouns	object pronouns	
I you he she it we they	me you him her it us them	**He** is nice. Mindy likes **him**. **I** am nice. Mindy likes **me**. **They** are nice. Mindy likes **them**.

5 **Find these phrases in the story. Who or what are the underlined words?**

1 Don't ask <u>her</u>. ______
2 I like <u>him</u>. ______
3 Can I have <u>it</u>? ______

Functions: making suggestions

6 2.30 **Listen and repeat.**

How about running / going / playing home? / to the beach? / tennis?

Let's run / go / play home. / to the beach. / tennis.

7 **Work with a friend. Make suggestions.**

A *Let's play tennis!*
B *OK then.*

A *How about playing tennis?*
B *Sorry, I can't.*

Fun Zone

8 2.31 **Listen and complete the rap. Then say the rap!**

you her them ~~me~~ him us

Football, football,
One two three,
It's time for the match!
Come with [1] *me* !

How about [2] ______?
How about [3] ______?
How about Mary,
Kate and Jim?

They like football,
Ask [4] ______ too,
Come with [5] ______!
It's fun with [6] ______!

5d DISCOVER SKILLS

Holiday Fun!

Reading

1 Look at the posters. What activities do you like?

2 2.32 Read and listen. Choose a camp for Milly and Jake.

How about a weekend at

Camp Robinson?

Do you like swimming and sailing in beautiful blue water?

Do you like painting beautiful pictures?

Do you like meeting new friends? **Yes! Yes! Yes!**

Camp Robinson is the camp for you!

Camp Crusoe

Let's have a weekend of fun!

What can I do there?

In summer, there's basketball and windsurfing.

In autumn, there's horse riding and golf.

There's skiing in winter.

In the evening, there's dancing and singing.

Camp Crusoe for all the family and for all your friends too!

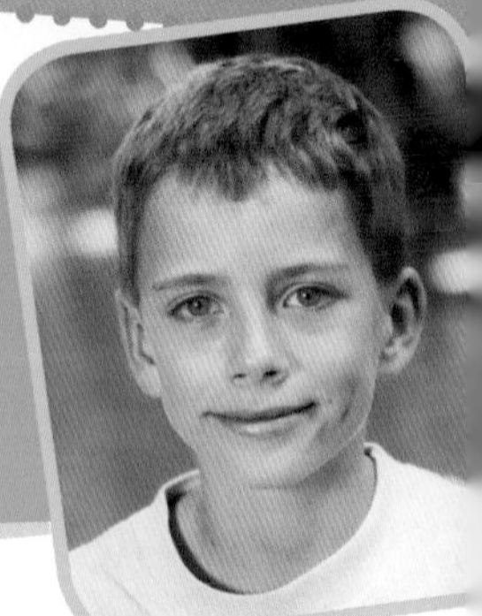

Jake loves meeting people. He likes all water sports but he hates winter sports. He doesn't like dancing.

Milly loves dancing and she likes singing too. She doesn't like painting and she hates swimming. She's in the basketball team at school. Horses are her favourite animals.

1 ________________ is a good camp for Milly.
2 ________________ is a good camp for Jake.

3 Read the posters. Find these things.

1 A water sport ____________
2 A ball game ____________
3 A winter sport ____________
4 A summer sport ____________

Listening

4 2.33 Listen to two boys talking. What sport are they talking about?

5 2.34 Listen again and complete.

WHAT? ________________

WHEN? ________________

WHERE? ________________

6 Look at Tom's diary. What sports does he like?

Tom's Diary

Monday	tennis
Tuesday	
Wednesday	
Thursday	tennis
Friday	
Saturday	
Sunday	

7 2.35 Listen and complete Tom's diary.

Speaking

Try this!

- Say the sentence in your head first.
- Practise the difficult words with a friend.

8 Ask your friends questions about sport. Write a name.

A *Do you like playing football?*
B *Yes, I do.*

9 Now tell the class.

A *He or she likes playing football but he or she doesn't like swimming.*
B *It's Gosia!*

Writing

10 Invent a camp for you! Make a poster.

- What is the name of the camp?
- What can you do there?
- Are there summer and winter sports?
- Are there fun activities in the evening?
- Who is the camp good for?

5e Let's Revise!

Words

1 Circle the words.

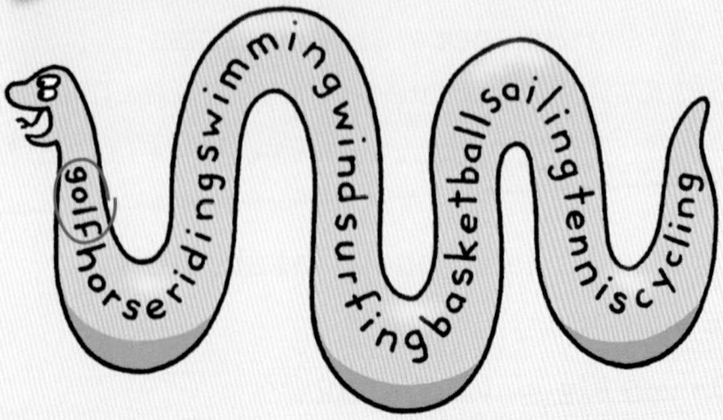

2 Write the activities from Exercise 1 in the correct column.

I play	I go
golf	*horse riding*

Grammar

3 Complete the sentences. Use *in*, *on* or *at*.

1 I play tennis *__in__* the morning.
2 He meets his friends ___ the weekend.
3 We go shopping ___ Saturday.
4 She gets up ___ seven o'clock.
5 They go on holiday ___ summer.
6 You study English ___ Monday.

4 Complete the sentences.

	Rupert	Laura
Cycling	✗	✓
Windsurfing	✓	✗
Swimming	✗	✗
Sailing	✓	✓

1 Laura likes …, but she doesn't …
2 Rupert … windsurfing, but …
3 Rupert and Laura like …
4 They don't …

5 Match and write.

What Who When Where

1 ______ does she live?
2 ______ is her favourite sport?
3 ______ does she train?
4 ______ is she?

Use the red letters to find the name! __________

6 Change the underlined words.

1 Gemma and Felix like cycling with <u>Ben</u>. *him*
2 They love windsurfing with <u>their friends</u>.
3 How about swimming with <u>Monica and me</u>?
4 Ben hates playing volleyball with <u>his sister</u>.

Pronunciation /w/ /v/

7 2.36 Listen and repeat.

On **W**ednesday
Veronica plays
volleyball and **W**endy
goes **w**indsurfing.

Functions

8 Work with a friend. Suggest five things to do this weekend.

A *Let's go swimming.*
B *How about playing cards?*

Checklist ✓

- I can talk about sports. ☐
- I can use question words. ☐
- I can use *like* + *-ing*. ☐
- I can name the seasons and times of day. ☐
- I can use object pronouns. ☐
- I can make suggestions. ☐

6 Detectives

Hi!
Our new webpage is about detectives.
Hey, look! There's a thief in town!

Discover Words

▶ places in town

1 2.37 Listen and follow the thief. Mark the trail on the map.

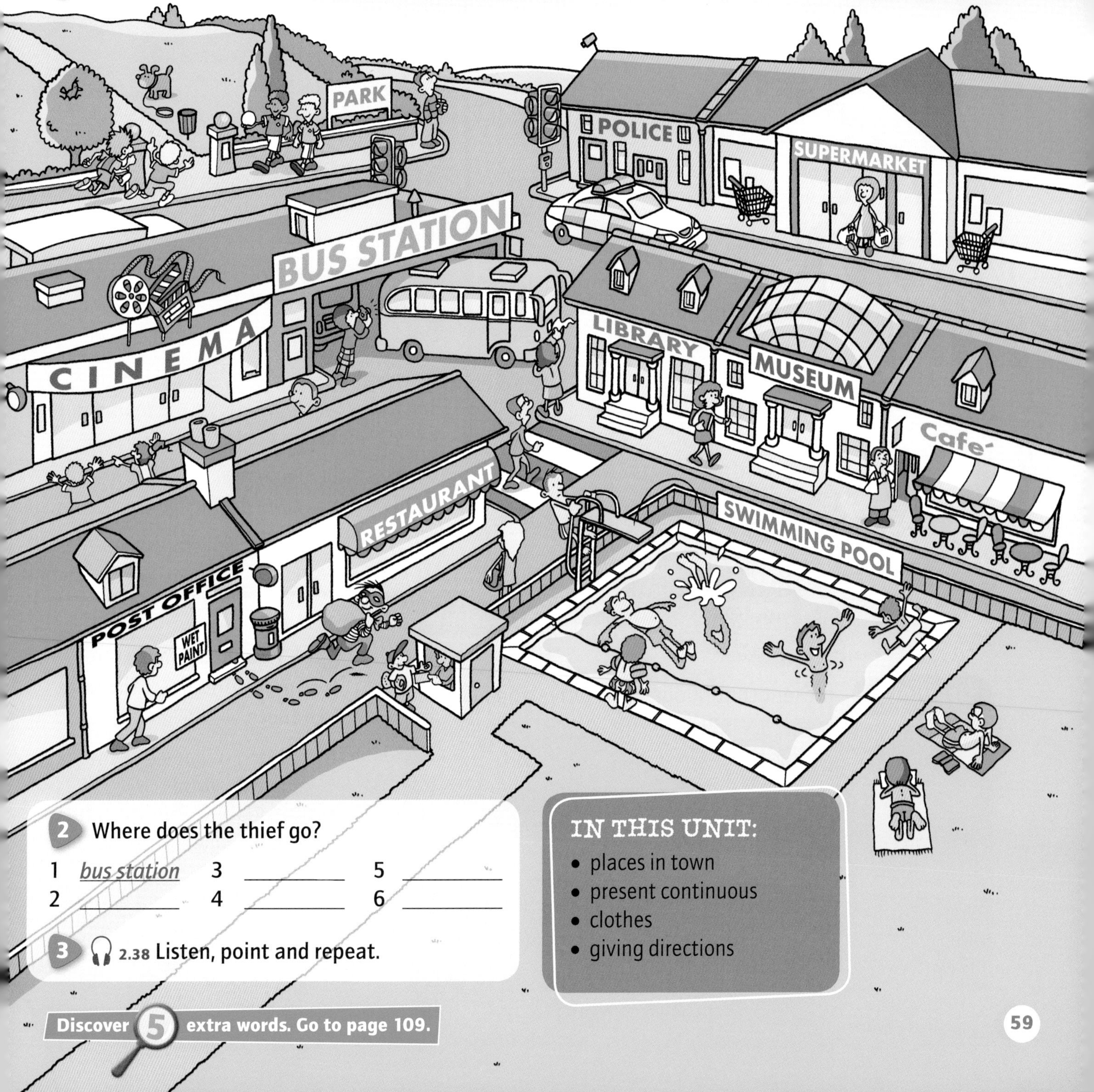

2 Where does the thief go?

1	*bus station*	3	________	5	________
2	________	4	________	6	________

3 2.38 Listen, point and repeat.

IN THIS UNIT:

- places in town
- present continuous
- clothes
- giving directions

Discover 5 extra words. Go to page 109.

6a It's a Mystery

1 Look at the picture. What is the story about? Who are the characters?

The Money Mystery

by Casey Storm

PART 1

Brad is behind a tree. He's talking to Mick on the phone.

Brad Mick, I'm in the park, but there's a problem.
Mick What is it, Brad?
Brad There are children here.
Mick What children?
Brad A boy and a girl. They've got a dog.
Mick Have they got the money?
Brad No, the dog's running to the tree. Oh no! Now they're stopping.
Mick Can they see the bag?
Brad Yes, and the girl's opening it. They're smiling.
Mick I'm not smiling, Brad. I'm not smiling at all.
Brad Oh no! Now they're looking at me!

The children's names are Bella and Eliot. They're sitting in a café. At the moment, they're talking about the money.

Eliot It's our money now.
Bella Don't be silly. Let's go to the police station.
Eliot No Bella, wait! Don't go!

Grammar present continuous: affirmative and negative

I	'm 'm not	talking	at the moment. now. today.
He She It	is isn't		
You We They	are aren't		

2 2.39 **Read and listen. True or false? Correct the false sentences.**

1 The dog is running at the moment. *false*
2 The dog is sitting near a tree.
3 At the moment Bella and Eliot are walking.
4 They're looking at a bag.
5 Eliot is opening the bag.
6 A man is talking to Bella and Eliot.

Watch Out!

smile → smiling
run → running
look → looking

3 2.40 Now read Part 2. Complete the story with the present continuous of the verbs in brackets. Listen and check.

PART 2

Mick Where are you now?
Brad [1] _'m following (follow) the girl.
Mick Has she got the money?
Brad Yes, she has. She [2] __________ (take) it to the police station!
Mick The police station? Oh no! Stop her!

Eliot is angry with Bella. He [3] __________ (sit) in the café and he [4] __________ (listen) to the news:

'The police [5] __________ (look for) a dangerous thief. He's tall, with brown hair and blue eyes.'

'The man behind the tree in the park!' Eliot thinks. 'Oh no! Bella!'

4 2.41 Listen to the description and tick the correct picture. How does the story end?

A

B

5 Make sentences. Which sentences describe picture A?

1 man / run. *A man is running.*
2 Bella / not smile.
3 a police officer / open the bag.
4 dog / not sit down.
5 Bella / not talk on the phone.
6 Eliot and Bella / feel happy.

6 Which ending is your favourite?

Speaking

7 Work with a friend. Student A, choose picture A or B. Student B, close your book and remember!

B *A police officer is talking to Bella …*

6b Is He Famous?

Felix Wow! There's Daniel Craig.
Monica You're joking! Where? What's he wearing?
Felix He's wearing a black T-shirt and jeans.
Ben Is he famous?
Felix Yes, he is. He's 007, the new James Bond.
Ben Really? Where is he?
Monica There! He's talking on his mobile phone.
Gemma That isn't Daniel Craig.
Felix Yes, it is.
Monica Oh no, he's going.
Felix Hey! His sunglasses are on the table.
Gemma Felix, what are you doing?
Felix I've got his sunglasses. Come on, Monica! Let's go!

(*a few minutes later*)

Felix Look! We've got his autograph.
Gemma No, you haven't. It says 'Thanks kids – Chris Smith'.
Felix No way!
Monica How embarrassing!

1 2.42 **Listen and read.**

2 **True or false? Correct the false sentences.**

1 Felix thinks the man is famous. ***true***
2 The man is talking to a friend at the café.
3 He isn't wearing sunglasses.
4 Gemma and Monica follow the man.
5 Felix has got Daniel Craig's autograph.

Talking Tips!

3 2.43 **Listen, repeat and match.**

1 You're joking!
2 How embarrassing!

A

B

Discover Words

clothes

4 2.44 **Label the clothes. Listen, check and repeat.**

trousers *2*   a jumper   a dress   a skirt   a coat   a hat   shorts   socks   shoes   jeans   a T-shirt   boots

5 **What are people wearing in the photo?**

Gemma is wearing a yellow dress.

6 **What are you wearing today?**

I'm wearing a …

Grammar present continuous: questions

Am	I **wearing** a T-shirt today?
Yes, I **am**. / No, I'**m not**.	
Are	you we **wearing** a T-shirt today? they
Yes, you **are**. / No, you **aren't**.	
Is	he she **wearing** a T-shirt today? it
Yes, she **is**. / No, she **isn't**.	
What **are** they **wearing**?	

Fun Zone

8 2.45 **Listen and circle Max.**

Speaking

7 **Write questions. Ask and answer with a friend.**

1 Felix drink / water?
Is Felix drinking water? No, he isn't.
2 Ben take / a photo?
3 Monica read / a magazine?
4 Ben and Gemma / talk to / the man?
5 the man sit / on a chair?

9 **Now describe another person in the photo. Your friend can guess.**

Writing

10 **Now write about one of the people.**

He's wearing … He's next to …

6c Earth Explorer

It's Friday and there's a school trip to a film studio.

1

2

3

4

5

6

Discover Words

▶ directions

1 🎧 2.46 **Match the directions with the pictures. Listen, check and repeat.**

go straight on *6*	turn left
go past	on the left
turn right	on the right

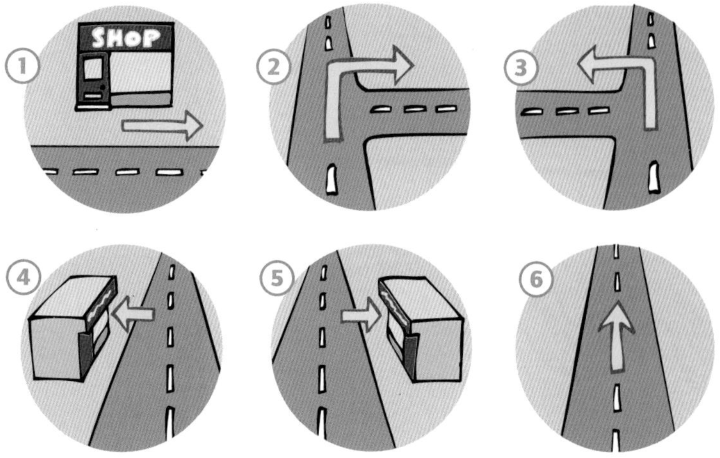

2 🎧 2.47 **Listen and read the Earth Explorer cartoon.**

3 Which pictures?

1 Fiz is wearing a hat.
Pictures 3, 4 and 5
2 Kit is opening a door.
3 Mindy is talking to Kit.
4 Kit is looking for studio 3.
5 A woman is following Fiz.
6 Kit is looking at Pamela.
7 Fiz is stopping a thief.

4 Help Fiz with his report. Find the sentences.

REPORT FROM EARTH

Today|we're|atafilmstudio.I'mfamo
ushere,butI'mnotaverygooddetec
tive.

Today we're ...

5 Act out the Earth Explorer cartoon with your friends.

Functions: giving directions

6 🎧 2.48 **Listen and read the dialogues. Follow the directions and complete the map.**

Kit Excuse me, I'm looking for the library.
You Turn right at the café, then go straight on. The library is on the left.

Kit Excuse me, where's the cinema?
You Turn left, then go past the park. The cinema is on the right.

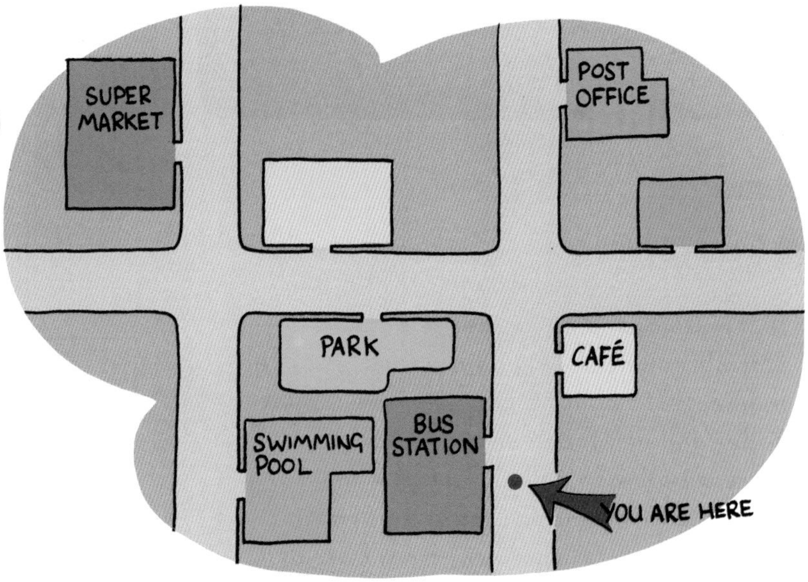

7 Work with a friend. Student A wants to go to the post office and the swimming pool. Student B wants to go to the café and the supermarket.

A *Excuse me, where's...*
B *Go straight on...*

6d Let's Revise!

Words

1 Circle the words.

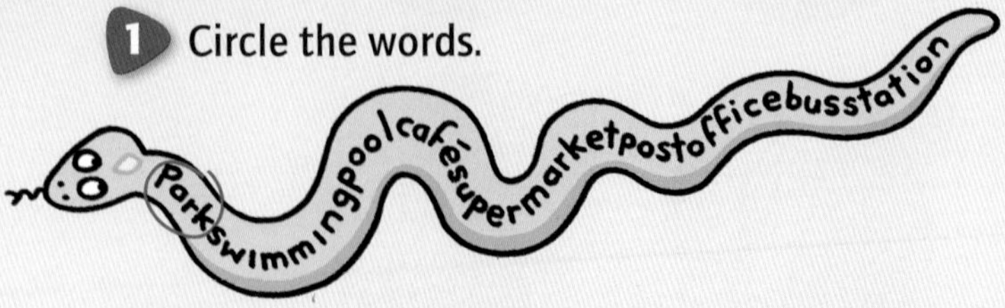

2 Look at the picture of superspy Alex Rider and his friend, Sabina. What are they wearing?

Grammar

3 Complete the text.

Hi, I'm Gina, and my favourite book is Stormbreaker. [1] I <u>'m reading</u> (read) it at the moment! It's about a spy. His name is Alex Rider and he's fourteen years old. In the story, a bad man called Darrius is following Alex and his friend Sabina. In this picture they [2] ________ (not run) from Darrius. Alex [3] __________ (help) Sabina. He [4] __________ (not talk) to her, and he [5] __________ (not smiling). Sabina [6] __________ (not look) at Alex. She [7] __________ (feel) scared. Alex Rider does lots of dangerous things.

4 Order the questions. Write the answers.

1 Gina reading what at the moment is?
What is Gina reading at the moment?
She's reading Stormbreaker.
2 following is Who Darrius?
3 running from Darrius Are Alex and Sabina?
4 What doing is Alex?
5 smiling Is Alex?
6 talking Are they?
7 Is feeling Sabina scared?

Pronunciation /ŋ/

5 2.49 Listen and repeat.

He's think**ing** and drink**ing** and sing**ing** in the street.

Functions

6 Follow the directions. Complete the gaps.

A: Excuse me, I'm looking for the __________.
B: Turn left and walk past the supermarket. Turn right at the library, then go straight on. The _________ is on the left.

Consolidation

7 2.50 **Listen and complete the dialogue.**

Gemma Hi, Monica. It's Gemma. [1] *What* are you doing?
Monica I'm with Ben. He's helping [2] _______ with Discovery Web. [3] _______ are you?
Gemma I'm at Fun Fashion. I'm [4] _______ for some new clothes.
Monica For the school party?
Gemma That's right.
Monica What are [5] _______ looking for?
Gemma I [6] _______ know.
Monica How [7] _______ a dress?
Gemma I [8] _______ wearing dresses.
Monica Or a skirt? You can wear my purple skirt.
Gemma Thanks, but I like [9] _______ jeans.
Monica [10] _______ about a new T-shirt then?
Gemma Hmm, there's a nice red T-shirt here and some funny green and red socks!
Monica Oh Gemma, you're joking!

Checklist ✓

I can name places in town.
I can use the present continuous.
I can describe clothes.
I can give and ask for directions.

Song

8 **Match the words with the pictures.**

clue *4* magnifying glass key puzzle

9 **Complete the song. Use the words from Exercise 8.**

I Spy

I spy,
With my little eye.
It's a mystery,
Can you help me find the [1] *key*.

I can use my [2] ___________,
To look for a clue that's from the past.
It's time to solve, it's time to find,
A mystery of a different kind.

Chorus
I spy (I spy),
With my little eye (with my little eye),
Can you give me a [3] ___________.
Can you tell me what to do.
I spy (I spy),
With my little eye (with my little eye).
It's a mystery.
Can you help me find the [4] ___________.

The missing piece of the [5] ___________,
May be right before your eyes.
A secret or a message that is,
Cleverly disguised.

10 2.51 **Listen, check and sing the song.**

6e Discover Culture

SPIES AND DETECTIVES

Ⓐ Sherlock Holmes is a great British detective. He's from London and his house is in Baker Street. Holmes is a tall, thin man and he is very clever. In this picture he's wearing a hat and he's looking for a clue.

There are sixty Sherlock Holmes stories. The stories are by Sir Arthur Conan Doyle and you can read them in sixty-three languages!

① 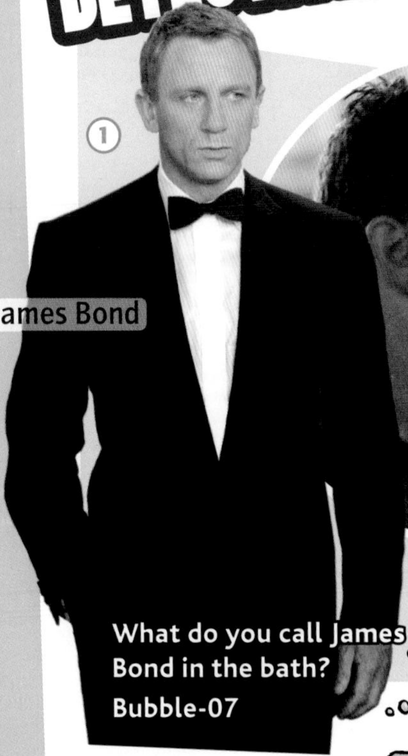
James Bond

② 
Ethan Hunt

③ 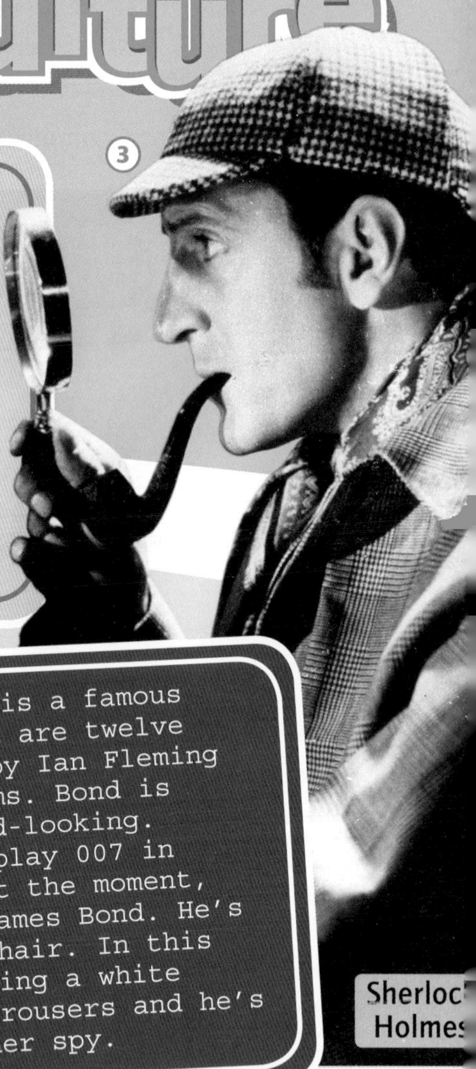
Sherlock Holmes

Ⓑ James Bond or 007 is a famous British spy. There are twelve James Bond books by Ian Fleming and twenty-one films. Bond is dangerous and good-looking. Different actors play 007 in different films. At the moment, Daniel Craig is James Bond. He's tall with blonde hair. In this picture he's wearing a white shirt and black trousers and he's looking for another spy.

What do you call James Bond in the bath?
Bubble-07

Reading

1 2.52 Read, listen and match the photos with the descriptions. There is one extra photo.

2 Read and match.

a James Bond
b Sherlock Holmes

Who …

1 wears a hat? b *Sherlock Holmes*
2 is very clever?
3 is in twenty-one films?
4 has got a house on Baker Street?
5 is dangerous?

Project

A Famous Spy

3 Think about a spy or detective. Complete a factfile like this. Tell your friend.

detective / spy	*Ethan Hunt*
appearance	*short brown hair brown eyes*
from	*USA*
your favourite film / story	*Mission Impossible 3*

4 Now write a paragraph. Use your ideas from the factfile.

7 Celebrations

Hi!
We're writing about celebrations today. When are your favourite celebrations?

Discover Words

▶ months

1 3.2 Complete the calendar. Listen, check and chant.

October May February ~~December~~ July September
April November ~~January~~ August March June

Calendar 2010

January
____
____
____
____
____
____
____
____
____
____
December

2 Which month?

1 I go on holiday in __________.
2 My birthday is in __________.
3 Christmas is in __________.

3 When is Monica's birthday?

It's in winter.
It's after Christmas.
It's a short month.
It's got eight letters.
____

4 Now write your own puzzle.

IN THIS UNIT:

- frequency adverbs
- present simple and present continuous
- dates
- talking about the weather

7a Happy Birthday!

Gemma Hey, Monica!

Monica Oh hi! I'm looking for a card for Ben. It's his birthday on Saturday.

Gemma Yes, you're right! I never remember birthdays!

Monica How about buying a present with me?

Gemma OK, but what? We often buy football things for Felix.

Monica I don't know. What about a CD?

Gemma That's a good idea. He likes rock music. He usually listens to McFly.

Monica But he's got all their music.

Gemma He sometimes listens to pop music too.

Monica How about a Shakira CD?

Gemma Yeah! Shakira CDs are always good. Let's buy one and listen to it today.

Monica That isn't fair, Gemma! It's for Ben. We aren't opening his presents now.

Gemma It's a joke, Monica! But it's my birthday in June …

Monica Oh Gemma!

1 3.3 **Listen and read.**

2 **True or false? Correct the false sentences.**

1 Monica and Gemma are in a café. *false*
2 It's Ben's birthday today.
3 Monica is buying Ben a card.
4 Ben doesn't like rock music.
5 Ben's got a lot of McFly CDs.
6 Gemma's birthday isn't in June.

Talking Tips!

3 3.4 **Listen, repeat and match.**

1 That isn't fair!
2 That's a good idea.

A

B

Grammar frequency adverbs

always	●●●●●
usually	●●●○
often	●●○○
sometimes	●○○○
never	○○○○

He **always** listens to Shakira.
He **usually** listens to McFly.
She **often** listens to rock music.
He **sometimes** listens to music.
I **never** remember birthdays.

4 **Look at the chart. Complete the sentences.**

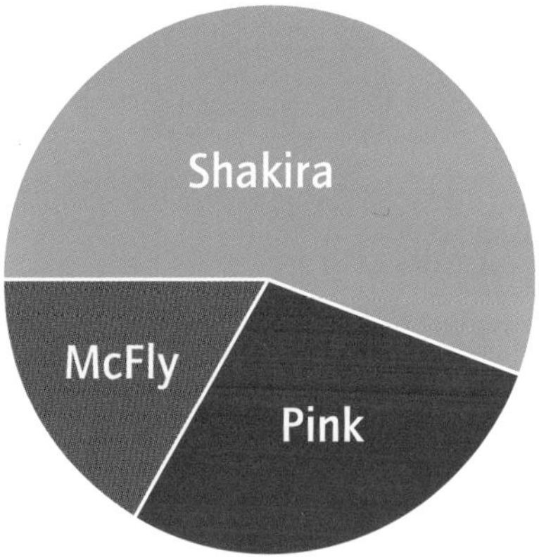

1 She _______ listens to Shakira.
2 She _______ listens to McFly.
3 She _______ listens to Pink.
4 She _______ listens to Coldplay.

5 **Write true sentences. Use a frequency adverb.**

1 I _______ have a party for my friends on my birthday.
2 We _______ dance to pop music at parties.
3 My mum _______ buys a birthday cake.
4 It is _______ cold on my birthday.
5 I _______ go to the park on my birthday.
6 I am _______ late for parties.

Watch Out!

He always listens to Shakira.
Shakira CDs are always good.

6 **Order the sentences.**

1 often / My best friend / rock music / listens to .
My best friend often listens to rock music.
2 always / I / parties / go to .
3 fun / usually / Parties / are .
4 birthdays / He / remembers / never .
5 Monica / cake / eats / sometimes .
6 happy on his birthday / Felix / always / is .

Listening

7 3.5 **Listen and tick. How does Jessie celebrate her birthday?**

	party	cards	presents	cake	ice cream
always			✓		
often					
usually					
sometimes					
never					

Speaking

8 **What about you? Work with a friend. Ask and answer the questions.**

1 Do you have a party on your birthday?
2 Do you have a cake?
3 Do you play games?
4 Do your friends buy presents for you?
5 Do you have cards?

Writing

9 **Now write about your friend's birthday.**

On Karolina's birthday, she usually ...

7b Let's Celebrate!

We've got some great pictures for Discovery Web this month. Look at these!

A

Hi, my name's Lee and today is Chinese New Year. What are we doing? We're celebrating of course! Every year we have a special street party. At the moment, people are watching a dragon in the street. Some people are playing the drums and my sister is dancing. We're wearing special clothes today.

Chinese New Year is usually in January or February but we never celebrate it on January 1st. This year it's on January 18th.

B

Hi, my name's Anna and I'm from Poland. Easter is my favourite celebration. On Easter Sunday we have a big family breakfast. We always have a basket of eggs on the table and there are special cakes too.

We sometimes celebrate Easter in March but it's usually in April. Today is April 27th and it's Easter Monday. All my friends are in the garden. Now they're throwing water at everyone! It's a very old tradition and its fun!

1 3.6 **Listen, read and complete the sentences.**

1. Lee is from *China*.
2. Chinese New Year is in ______ or ______.
3. Anna's favourite celebration is ______.
4. Anna's family have a basket of ______.
5. At the moment Anna's friends are throwing ______.

Grammar present simple and present continuous

present simple

Every year we have a special street party.
We **sometimes** celebrate Easter in March.

present continuous

At the moment, people are watching a dragon.
We're wearing special clothes **today**.
Now they're throwing water.

2 Read and circle the correct words.

1 We celebrate / are celebrating Christmas every year.
2 At the moment I buy / am buying presents.
3 Every Christmas we go / are going to London.
4 Now we write / are writing cards.
5 We don't have / aren't having a party every December.

3 Read and complete. Use the present simple or present continuous of the verbs in brackets.

1 Every year at New Year we *have* (have) a party.
2 Today I ____________ (buy) presents.
3 At the moment we ____________ (wear) party clothes.
4 We ____________ (not wear) party clothes every day.
5 Now we ____________ (listen) to pop music.

4 Order the questions. Ask and answer with a friend.

1 always / Do you / New Year / celebrate ?
Do you always celebrate New Year?
2 wear new clothes / usually / Do you / at parties ?
3 now / celebrating a festival / Are you ?
4 to music / listening / Are you ?
5 buy presents / Do you / often ?
6 at the moment / writing a card / Are you ?

Discover Words

ordinal numbers

5 3.7 Listen, chant and match.

1st	sixth	7th	twelfth
2nd	second	8th	tenth
3rd	fourth	9th	eleventh
4th	first	10th	eighth
5th	third	11th	ninth
6th	fifth	12th	seventh

Watch Out!

November 5th

November the fifth!

6 Look at the calendar. Write the date.

1 Mum's birthday is on *March 1st*.
2 There's a football match on ____________.
3 Ben's party is on ____________.
4 Dad's birthday is on ____________.
5 Easter Sunday is on ____________.

When's your birthday?
It's on ________.

March		
1 Mum's birthday	2	3
4	5 Football Match	6
7	8	9
10 Ben's party	11	12
13	14	15
16	17	18
19	20	21
22	23 Dad's birthday	24
25	26	27
28	29	30
31 Easter Sunday		

Fun Zone

7 Play word tennis!

A *one!*
B *first!*

7c Earth Explorer

1

Kids: Trick or treat?
Mum: Here, have a treat.
Kids: Sweets! Thanks.

2

Fiz: Why are you wearing strange clothes?
Kit: It's Hallowe'en, Fiz. People usually wear scary clothes.
Bandit: ... and play tricks ... Ha! Ha!

3

Kit: Come on. Let's get some sweets.
Fiz: But I'm not scary.
Kit: You're scary for people on my planet!
Girl: Hey, he's spooky!

4

Fiz: Brrr! It's cold tonight and it's foggy. Can we go home?
Kit: No, look! There's a house.

5

Fiz: What's that?
Kit: It's windy, that's all. ... Hello, hello?

6

Fiz: Aaagghh! Help!
Kit: Ha! Ha! It's OK Fiz. It's Bandit. It's a trick.
Bandit: I love Hallowe'en!

1 3.8 **Listen and read.**

2 **Answer the questions.**

1 What festival are the children celebrating?
Hallowe'en
2 What are the children wearing?
3 Is Fiz wearing scary clothes?
4 Is it cold on Hallowe'en night?
5 Who plays a trick on Fiz?

3 **Break the code! Write the report.**

REPORT FROM EARTH

I don't …

4 **Act out the Earth Explorer cartoon with your friends.**

Discover Words

weather

5 3.9 **Match the words with the pictures. Listen, check and repeat.**

It's hot. *4* It's cold. It's sunny. It's cloudy.
It's windy. It's foggy. It's raining. It's snowing.

Functions: talking about the weather

6 3.10 **Listen and repeat.**

A *What's the weather like?*
B *It's sunny.*

7 **Work with a friend.**

A: Draw weather symbols for places 1–4.
B: Draw weather symbols for places 5–8.
Ask about your friend's places and draw.

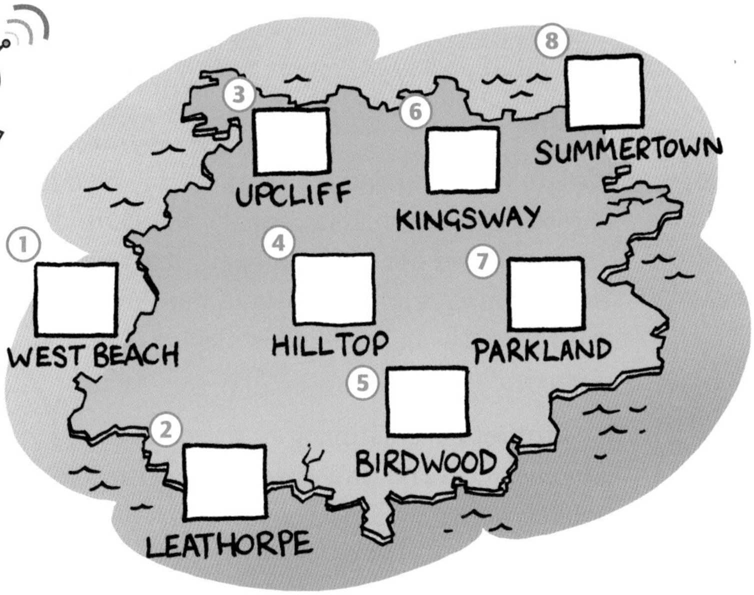

A *What's the weather like in Kingsway?*
B *It's raining!*

Fun Zone

8 3.11 **Listen and complete.**

Is it [1] *hot*?
Is it [2] ________?
Is it [3] ________ today?

It's great,
It's spring,
It's the first of May!

Is it [4] ________?
Is it [5] ________?
Or is there [6] ________?

Is it [7] ________?
Is it [8] ________?
Listen again!

9 3.12 **Listen and rap!**

Discover 5 extra words. Go to page 109.

DISCOVER SKILLS 7d

Festivals

Reading

1 3.13 **Listen and read Gabriel's diary. What is he celebrating?**

Monday March 4th

It's hot, it's sunny and it's the first day of the Carnival! Yippeee!! This year it's the 150th Carnival so we are having a really big party. There is always lots of music in the street and today my uncle's band is playing. They're fantastic!

My brothers are listening to the band and dancing. Mum and Dad aren't working today. Nobody works in Carnival week and nobody goes to school. It's great! At the moment Mum's cooking special food for the street party. Granny's helping her. We always have a Carnival Queen. She's usually very pretty and wears a beautiful long dress. My sister is feeling sad today. She's got a new dress but she isn't the Carnival Queen – bad luck, Nancy!

2 **Read the diary again and answer the questions.**

1 What's the date?
2 What's the weather like?
3 What is Gabriel's mum doing?
4 Describe the Carnival Queen.

Listening

3 🎧 3.14 **Listen and circle the words you hear.**

Japan Holi February water snow
colours dress cold March
dinosaur coat (India)

4 🎧 3.15 **Listen and complete. Use words from Exercise 3 that are not in a circle.**

Holi Festival, India

1 Hi, I'm Rie from ______.
2 We are celebrating the snow festival. It usually starts on the first Monday of ______.
3 Every year people come and see the ______ buildings.
4 It is usually very ______ but we always have hot food and drinks.
5 In the photo I am looking at a ______.
6 I am wearing a big ______ because it's very cold.

Speaking

5 **Describe a photo!**
Work with a friend.
Throw a coin.

Heads = say a sentence about picture A
Tails = say a sentence about picture B

A *People celebrate Holi in March.*
B *In this picture they are celebrating …*

Snow Festival, Japan

Writing

6 **Imagine that today is your favourite celebration. Write a page in your diary. Use Gabriel's diary to help you. Include:**

- the date
- the food
- the clothes
- the weather
- the activities

Try this!

- Write your diary. Then read it.
- Check your grammar and spelling.
- Write it again.

How does a car celebrate its birthday?
It goes to a car-nival!

7e Let's Revise!

Words

1 Find the months.

1 SAUGUT *August*
2 EBFRYUAR
3 PIRAL
4 UENJ
5 YJNAURA
6 OBMNVERE

2 Write the dates.

1 It's the twenty-second. *22nd*
2 It's the thirty-first.
3 It's the eleventh.
4 It's the third.
5 It's the twentieth.
6 It's the twelfth.

Grammar

3 Order the sentences.

1 always celebrate / in December / People / Christmas.
2 in April / but sometimes. / Easter / is usually / in March.
3 Hallowe'en / never celebrate / People / in June.

4 Read and circle.

Hi! It's my birthday today and we [1] **have / are having** a party. At the moment [2] **I'm standing / stand** in the garden. My favourite music [3] **plays / is playing** and people [4] **are singing / sing** 'Happy Birthday'. I [5] **don't usually have / am not usually having** a party and I [6] **don't always get / am not always getting** a birthday cake but today is different. I've got a big birthday cake and lots of presents!

Pronunciation /ɪ/ /iː/

5 3.16 Listen and repeat.

Christine is six at Christmas but I'm sixteen at Hallowe'en.

Functions

6 Order the question. Write the answers.

the / What's / like / weather ?

____

1 *It's raining!*
2
3
4
5
6

Checklist ✓

I can use frequency adverbs. ☐
I can use the present simple and present continuous. ☐
I can talk about dates. ☐
I can talk about the weather. ☐

8 School

Hi! Our subject this month is school. Do you like school? I do – it's fun!

Discover Words

▶ school subjects

1 🎧 3.17 **Listen, repeat and match.**

English *8* computer studies science art history French
P.E. (physical education) geography music maths

2 🎧 3.18 **Listen and write the subject.**

1 *music*
2
3
4
5
6

IN THIS UNIT:

- school subjects
- *was / were*
- time expressions
- past simple regular
- talking about feelings

Discover 5 extra words. Go to page 109.

8a A Bad Day

Yesterday was Tuesday. It was a bad day!

Ben's joke wasn't funny.

History was OK, but my teacher wasn't happy.

Then at lunchtime ...

And in the afternoon ...

1 3.19 **Read and listen. Tick the subjects Gemma has on Tuesday.**

science	✓	history	☐
music	☐	geography	☐
maths	☐	French	☐

Talking Tips!

2 3.20 **Listen, repeat and match.**

1 Move over!
2 Don't worry!

(A)

(B)

Grammar	*to be:* past simple	
I He She It	**was** **wasn't**	at school yesterday.
You We They	**were** **weren't**	at school last week.

3 **Write the dates, days, months or years.**

yesterday   last Friday   last year
last month   last night

Yesterday was Monday.
Last Friday was September 5th.

4 **Complete the sentences. Use *was*, *wasn't*, *were* and *weren't*.**

1 Gemma's first lesson *was* science.
2 Gemma and Ben ______ in the same class for science.
3 Gemma's history homework ______ in her bag.
4 The chips ______ Monica's.
5 After school, the other people in the band ______ in the music room.
6 Gemma ______ happy.

Grammar	*to be:* past simple questions		
Was	I he she it	funny?	Yes, I **was**. No, it **wasn't**.
Were	you we they	funny?	Yes, we **were**. No, they **weren't**.

5 **Complete the questions and answers.**

1 *Were* Felix and Ben at school last week? ✓
Yes, they were.
2 _____ Gemma and Monica at the library last night? ✗
3 _____ Ben at the park yesterday? ✓
4 _____ Felix and Gemma at the swimming pool last Saturday? ✗
5 _____ Monica at Ben's house last Friday? ✓

Speaking

6 **Ask and answer about your weekend.**

shops   park   library   swimming pool
cinema   a friend's house   school

A *Were you at the shops last Saturday?*
B *Yes, I was. / No, I wasn't.*

8b A Lesson For Life

www.DiscoveryWeb/Tilly

Do you always listen in class?
Read about Tilly Smith and a lesson that helped lots of people.

In December 2004, Tilly Smith was in Phuket with her mum and dad. It was her first holiday in Thailand and the family was very happy. On December 26th they were on Mai Khao beach when the sea disappeared. It was strange and people walked to the sea and watched. Tilly watched too, but she wasn't happy. She remembered a geography lesson at school. In the lesson they studied tsunamis. Tsunamis are very big, dangerous waves. Before they crash on the beach, the sea disappears. Tilly shouted. People stopped and listened. They hurried from the beach.

Then, the tsunami arrived. It was a tragedy for lots of people in Asia, but the people on Mai Khao beach were safe.

Email comments on this week's story to
Monica@DiscoveryWeb

1 3.21 **Listen and read the story. Which lesson did Tilly remember?**

French lesson ☐
history lesson ☐
geography lesson ☐

Grammar past simple: affirmative

I You He She It We They	watch**ed** the sea. stud**ied** tsunamis. stop**ped** and listen**ed**. lik**ed** geography lessons.

2 3.22 **Listen and repeat. Listen to the different endings.**

stud**ied** shout**ed** stop**ped**

Watch Out!

stop → stopped
study → studied
like → liked

3 3.23 **Underline the past simple verbs in the text. Listen, check and repeat.**

4 **Complete the sentences. Use the past simple.**

1 Tilly Smith *studied* (study) tsunamis at school.
2 She ______ (arrive) in Thailand with her mum and dad in December.
3 On December 26th, the sea on Mai Khao beach ______ (disappear).
4 The people on the beach ______ (watch).
5 Tilly ______ (shout) and they ______ (listen) to her.
6 In England, Tilly ______ (talk) to her friends about the tsunami.

5 **Complete the story. Use the verbs in the past simple.**

stop talk hurry look arrive ~~walk~~

When I [1] walked to school on Monday, I [2] ______ at a shop for some sweets. I [3] ______ to a friend in the shop. After five minutes, she [4] ______ at her watch. It was ten past nine – we were late! We [5] ______ to school and [6] ______ at quarter past nine. We were lucky. The teacher was late too!

6 **Read the comments. Circle the correct answer.**

Tilly is lucky / amazing / boring / great.

Here are some comments on this week's web story:

Before Tilly's story, I didn't like geography. I like it now. Geography isn't boring – it's great!
Kieron, Class 5c

People listened to Tilly. They didn't stay on the beach. They were lucky Tilly was there. She's amazing!
Sean, Class 4a

Grammar past simple: negative

I You He She It We They	**didn't**	**listen.** **walk.**

7 **Underline the past simple negative in Exercise 6.**

8 **Complete the sentences. Use the past simple.**

1 Tilly's family *didn't stay* (not stay) at home for Christmas.
2 She ____________ (not like) the food in Thailand.
3 I ____________ (not have) a holiday last year.
4 We ____________ (not talk) to the man on the plane.
5 You ____________ (not write) any postcards.

9 **Tick the sentences that are true for you. Rewrite the false sentences.**

1 My mum and dad visited Thailand last year.
My mum and dad didn't visit Thailand last year.
2 We studied geography last Friday.
3 My maths homework disappeared last night.
4 I remembered my school books yesterday.
5 I watched a film about tsunamis last weekend.
6 We walked to school last week.

Fun Zone

10 **Work with two friends. Say what you did yesterday. Remember what your friends did.**

A *Yesterday I walked to school.*
B *Yesterday I walked to school and studied maths.*
C *Yesterday I walked to school, studied maths and …*

What's a snake's favourite subject? hiss-story!

8c Earth Explorer

On Wednesday afternoon Kit has science.

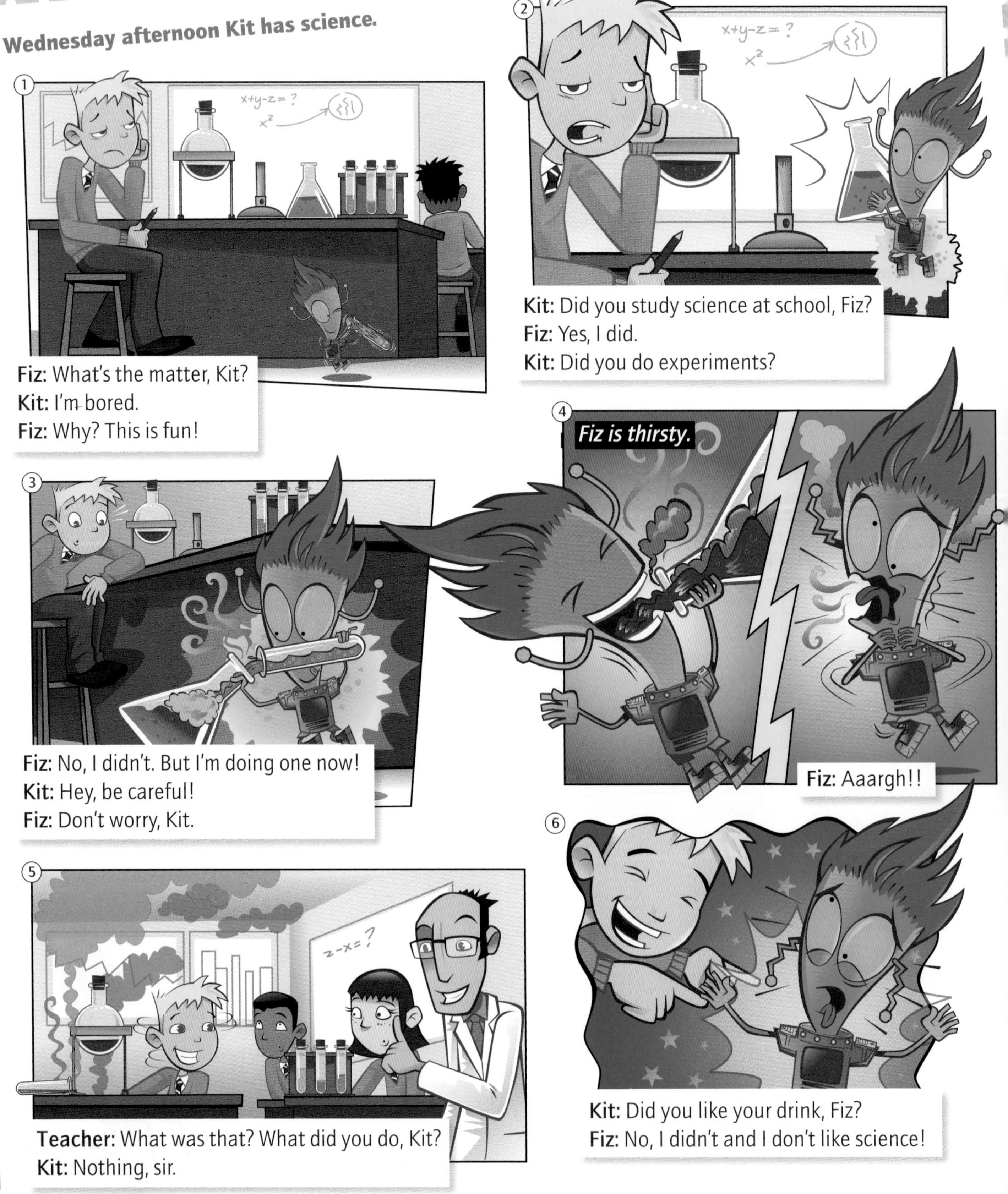

1 3.24 **Listen and read.**

2 **True or false?**

1 Kit likes science. *false*
2 Fiz studied science at school.
3 He did experiments at school.
4 Fiz's drink was disgusting.
5 The teacher didn't see Fiz.

3 **Help Fiz with his report. Find the sentences.**

REPORT FROM EARTH

I|was|atKit'sschooltoday. Westudied sciencebutIwasn'tcareful.
I was…

4 **Act out the Earth Explorer cartoon with your friends.**

Grammar past simple: questions

Did	I you he she it we they	**listen?** **run?** **walk?**
Yes, we **did**. / No, we **didn't**.		
What **did** you **study**?		

5 **Order the questions. Write the answers.**

1 you / Did / last night / watch a film ? ✓
Did you watch a film last night?
Yes, I did.
2 Did / last week / play tennis / you ? ✓
3 it / rain / Did / yesterday ? ✓
4 phone your friends / Did / you / last night ? ✗
5 last year / Did / you / study French ? ✗

Speaking

6 **Ask a friend the questions in Exercise 5.**

A *Did you watch a film last night?*
B *Yes, I did. / No, I didn't.*

Discover Words

feelings

7 3.25 **Listen, repeat and match.**

1	~~bored~~	3	~~worried~~	5	~~hungry~~	7	sad
2	scared	4	thirsty	6	tired	8	angry

A ______ B ______ C ______ D *worried*

E ______ F *hungry* G *bored* H ______

Functions: talking about feelings

8 3.26 **Listen and repeat.**

What's the matter?
I'm bored / angry / hungry / sad

Fun Zone

9 **Work with a friend. Mime a feeling and guess.**

A *What's the matter?*
(B mimes the feeling.)
A *You're hungry!*
B *That's right / wrong.*

8d Let's Revise!

Words

1 Match the word halves. What are the school subjects?

1	geog	ench
2	his	sic
3	mu	ence
4	sci	lish
5	ma	raphy
6	Eng	tory
7	Fr	ths

2 Complete the puzzle. Use the red letters to say how Fiz feels.

1	T	H	I	R	S		Y	
2		W	O	R	R		E	D
3			S	C			E	D
4			B		R		D	
5				S				

Grammar

3 What happened last night? Read and complete. Use the past simple.

Last night three men [1] *were* (be) in our school. They [2] ______ (walk) into our class with a big bag. Well, I was behind the cupboard. I [3] ______ (stop) my work and I [4] ______ (not move). I [5] ______ (listen) to the men. They [6] ______ (not talk), they shouted. I [7] ______ (be) scared! After half an hour they [8] ______ (disappear). I looked at the classroom. The computers [9] ______ (not be) there and the clock wasn't there. I phoned the police. Then the teacher arrived. 'Oh Jimmy!' she said. 'The men are painters! They are painting the classroom today!'

4 Order the questions. Write the answers.

1 Jimmy at school Was last night ?
Was Jimmy at school last night? Yes, he was.
2 strange men in the classroom Were ?
3 Jimmy Was under the chair ?
4 shout Did the men ?
5 Was scared Jimmy ?
6 phone Did Jimmy the police ?

5 Answer the questions.

1 Was it your birthday yesterday?
No, it wasn't. It was my birthday last July.
2 Did you study English last Saturday?
3 Was it cold last night?
4 Were you ten last year?
5 Was it sunny yesterday?
6 Did you listen to music last night?
7 Did you play football last week?

Pronunciation /t/ /d/ /ɪd/

6 3.27 Listen and repeat.

We walk**ed** and talk**ed** and play**ed** all day,
Ed arriv**ed** and shout**ed**, 'Hey!'

Functions

7 Circle the correct word.

What's the matter?

1 I'm bored / scared.

2 I'm angry / tired.

3 I'm thirsty / hungry.

4 I'm bored / sad.

Consolidation

8 3.28 Listen and complete the dialogue.

Felix Hello?
Monica Hi, Felix. Is Gemma there? She [1] *wasn't* at the football match. I [2] ______ for her.
Felix Gemmaaa!!
Gemma Hello?
Monica Hi, Gemma. You [3] ______! Where were you?
Gemma Sorry Monica. I [4] ______ in the library all evening. I [5] ______ my history project!
Monica But it's for Friday. Oh Gemma, you [6] ______ listen!
Gemma Yes, I [7] ______. It's for Friday 13th.
Monica No, Friday 20th!
Gemma Oh no! Did you [8] ______ the match then?
Monica No I [9] ______. It [10] ______ and I was cold so I didn't go.
Gemma What are you [11] ______ now?
Monica I [12] ______ my history project!

Song

9 3.29 Listen and complete the song. Then listen and sing.

play where don't ~~doing~~ shoes party

Celebrate

Stop what you're [1] *doing*
Right away
There's no time to work
'Cos it's time to [2] ______
Grab your dancing [3] ______
And your [4] ______ hat
Come along and join us
Get to [5] ______ it's at

Chorus
There's no need to wait
Let's Celebrate
Hurry, [6] ______ be late
Let's Celebrate
CELEBRATE
CELEBRATE
CELEBRATE

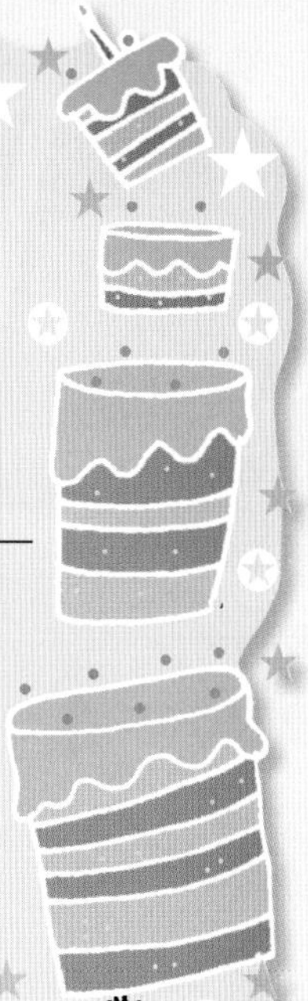

Checklist ✓

I can talk about school subjects. ☐
I can use *was / were*. ☐
I can use time expressions. ☐
I can use the past simple regular. ☐
I can talk about feelings. ☐

8e Discover Culture

Megan

Hillside School

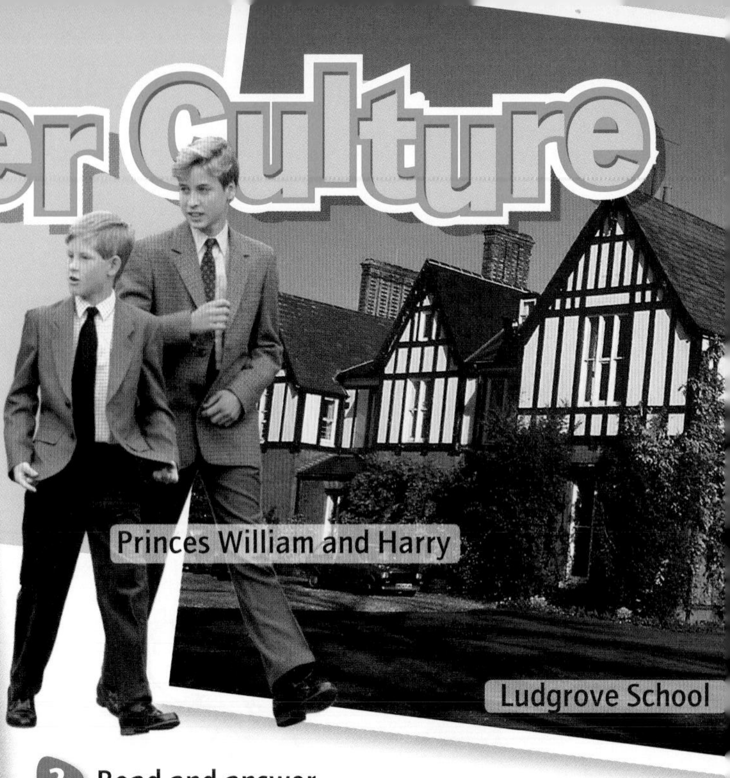
Princes William and Harry

Ludgrove School

Reading

1 3.30 Read and complete. Use these numbers. Listen and check.

~~five~~ nine three six twelve three ten

Hi! I'm Megan. My school is called Hillside. We start school when we are [1] *five* and stay for [2] ______ years. Then we go to secondary school. There are [3] ______ terms in the school year. The autumn term starts in September and finishes in December. The spring term finishes in April and the summer term finishes in July.
My school day starts at [4] ______ o'clock in the morning and finishes at half past [5] ______. Our class teacher, Miss Hay, teaches English, maths, history and geography. We have music, P.E. and computer studies too. There is a break in the morning, then we have lunch at [6] ______ o'clock and another break at [7] ______ past two. We have homework at the weekend.

2 Read and answer.

Prince William and his brother Harry were at a very different school. They were at Ludgrove. They started when they were eight and stayed for five years. There weren't any girls there and they didn't finish at half past three … they lived there!

1 Was Ludgrove a school for girls?
2 Did the children start when they were five?
3 Did they go home at half past three?

Project

My School

3 Ask and answer the questions with a friend.

1 What's the name of your school?
2 What time does your school start?
3 What subjects do you study?
4 Are there any breaks?
5 Do you have homework? When?

4 Now draw a picture of your school and write about it.

My School is called Tower Road. We start school …

9 Entertainment

Our Discovery Web subject this month is entertainment! Which of these is your favourite?

Discover Words

entertainment

1 3.31 Read and match. Listen and check.

concert *4* exhibition musical TV programme play film

ABC CINEMA
Superman – 7.30 p.m.

1

2

Strand Theatre
The Lion King
23rd May–15th June
A fantastic show with great songs.

3

The Royal Theatre
Shakespeare's Romeo and Juliet. All summer.

Pop in the park
The *Arctic Tigers* are at Summer Park.
Saturday 12–4 p.m.

5

New Art
Pictures by young artists.
The Art Café, 30th June.

BBC1 The Simpsons

6

2 3.32 Listen. What are they doing?

1 *They're watching a TV programme.*
2
3
4
5
6

IN THIS UNIT:
- entertainment
- past simple irregular
- opinion adjectives
- sequencers
- ordering events

Show Time!

1 3.33 Listen and read.

Last week we went to London with our school. We saw the musical GREASE! Lots of mums and dads came too.

The story was about a girl called Sandy. She met a boy on holiday. His name was Danny and Sandy really liked him. But after the holiday, Danny was different. His friends at school didn't like Sandy so Danny wasn't nice to her. Sandy was sad. But of course everyone was happy in the end.

Here's what YOU think:

It was great! I liked the music and the clothes were cool too. We had great fun!
Laura, Class 3b.

Mum took me in the car and we were late. We didn't see the start, but I loved it. Danny was very good-looking.
Holly, Class 2c.

It was fantastic! I really liked the cars and the songs. My mum and my brother were there, but my dad didn't come. Bad luck, Dad!
Jordan, Class 5a.

2 True or false?

1 Children from Ben's school were at a film last week. *false*
2 It was about a boy and a girl.
3 The boy was good-looking.
4 There wasn't any music.
5 Lots of mums and dads were there.

Grammar past simple: irregular

I You He She It We They	**saw** **didn't see**	the show.
	went **didn't go**	to the park.

 Discover 5 extra words. Go to page 109.

3 Find the past simple verbs in the text and complete.

present	past
go	w*en*t
see	s_w .
is	_ _s
meet	m_ _
have	_ _d
take	_ _ _k
come	c_m_

4 Put the verb into the affirmative past form.

1 Yesterday Monica *went* (go) to the theatre.
2 She ______ (see) a new musical.
3 It ______ (be) about a boy called Matteo.
4 He ______ (come) to England.
5 He ______ (meet) a girl called Daisy.
6 They ______ (have) lots of adventures.
7 Monica ______ (take) photos of the actors.

5 Put the verbs in the negative past form.

1 Ben *didn't go* (not go) to the theatre, he went to the cinema.
2 They _____ (not see) a musical, they saw a film.
3 It _____ (not be) about children, it was about animals.
4 Ben _____ (not like) the film. He was bored and hungry.
5 He _____ (not take) sweets to the cinema, he took money for ice cream.
6 The cinema _____ (not have) any ice cream.

What do cows do at the weekend?
They go to moosicals!

6 Read and complete with the correct verb in the past simple.

be have see ~~go~~ meet not like

Yesterday I [1] *went* to an exhibition. It [2] __________ about robots. I [3] __________ my friend Lucy there. We [4] __________ lots of amazing things. The robots were very clever. One of them [5] __________ twelve arms. I loved the exhibition but Lucy [6] __________ it. She was bored so we went home early.

Writing

7 Imagine and write!

Yesterday I went to ________.
I met ________ there.
It was about ________.
________ came too.
He/She ________ it but I ________ it.
It was great. / I was bored.

Fun Zone

8 Play past simple tennis!

A *Go!*
B *Went!*

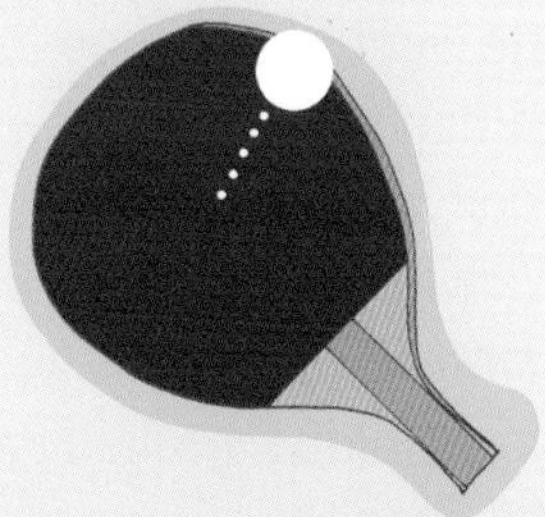

9b Super Films!

Monica Hi, Felix. What are you doing?
Felix Oh, hi! I'm looking for the DVD of *Smallville*. Gemma saw it last night, but I was at a football match. Did you see it?
Monica No, I didn't. Mum went out and I didn't have my key.
Felix Oh no. Where did she go?
Monica She went to the shops. I waited in the garden for an hour. It was so boring!
Felix Poor you!
Monica Wait a minute. I think Ben recorded *Smallville* last night.
Felix No, he didn't. I called him. He recorded the wrong programme.
Monica What was it?
Felix It was *Cook for your pet*.
Monica Great! We can go to his house for dinner then!
Felix Oh no! Yuk!

1 3.34 **Listen and read.**

2 **Complete with the correct name.**

Gemma ~~Felix~~ Monica Monica's mum Ben

1 <u>*Felix*</u> is looking for a DVD.
2 ____________ watched *Smallville* last night.
3 ____________ went to the shops.
4 ____________ waited in the garden.
5 ____________ recorded a programme about pet food.

Talking Tips!

3 3.35 **Listen, repeat and match.**

1 Poor you!
2 Wait a minute.

A

B

Grammar past simple irregular: questions

Did	I you he she it we they	**go** to the shop? **see** it?
Yes, we **did**. / No, we **didn't**.		
Where **did** you **go**? What **did** we **see**?		

4 Order the questions. Write the answers.

1 a DVD / watch / Did you / last night ?
Did you watch a DVD last night?
2 meet your friends / last / Did you / week ?
3 in the afternoon / call your friends / Did you ?
4 Did your friends / year / last / see a musical ?
5 on Saturday / to the theatre / go / Did your family ?
6 go / Did your mum / to the cinema / yesterday ?

5 3.36 Complete. Listen and check.

About Smallville

Jonathan and Martha [1] *didn't have* (not have) any children. One day, they [2] ___________ (see) something in their garden. It [3] ___________ (be) a baby boy.
He [4] ___________ (come) from the Planet Krypton. They [5] ___________ (take) the baby and they called him Clark. Clark [6] ___________ (go) to school in Smallville. Then he lived in Metropolis.

What is Clark's other name?

6 Write the answers.

1 How many children did Jonathan and Martha have?
They didn't have any children.
2 What did they see in their garden?
3 Where did the baby come from?
4 What did they call the baby?
5 Where did he go to school?

Discover Words

opinion adjectives

7 3.37 Listen and repeat.

1 fantastic
2 funny
3 terrible
4 exciting
5 boring
6 interesting
7 scary

Listening

8 3.38 Listen and match the films to the adjectives in Exercise 7.

① King Kong *4*
② Batman
③ Charlotte's Web
④ Garfield
⑤ Superman
⑥ Pirates of the Caribbean
⑦ Ice Age

Speaking

9 Work with a friend. Imagine you saw a film last night. Ask and answer. Use words from Exercise 7.

A Did you see ___________ last night?
B Yes, it was …

9c Earth Explorer

Kit is watching a film.

1 3.39 **Listen and read.**

2 **Answer the questions.**

1 What is Kit watching? *TV*
2 Why are the aliens dangerous?
3 Is Fiz scary?
4 Did the aliens go home?

3 **Break the code! Write the report.**

4 **Act out the Earth Explorer cartoon with your friends.**

Functions: ordering events

5 3.40 **Listen and repeat.**

First they watched our planet.
Then they came to Earth.
After that they saw Bandit.
Finally they went home.

6 3.41 **Work with a friend. Order the pictures. Listen and check.**

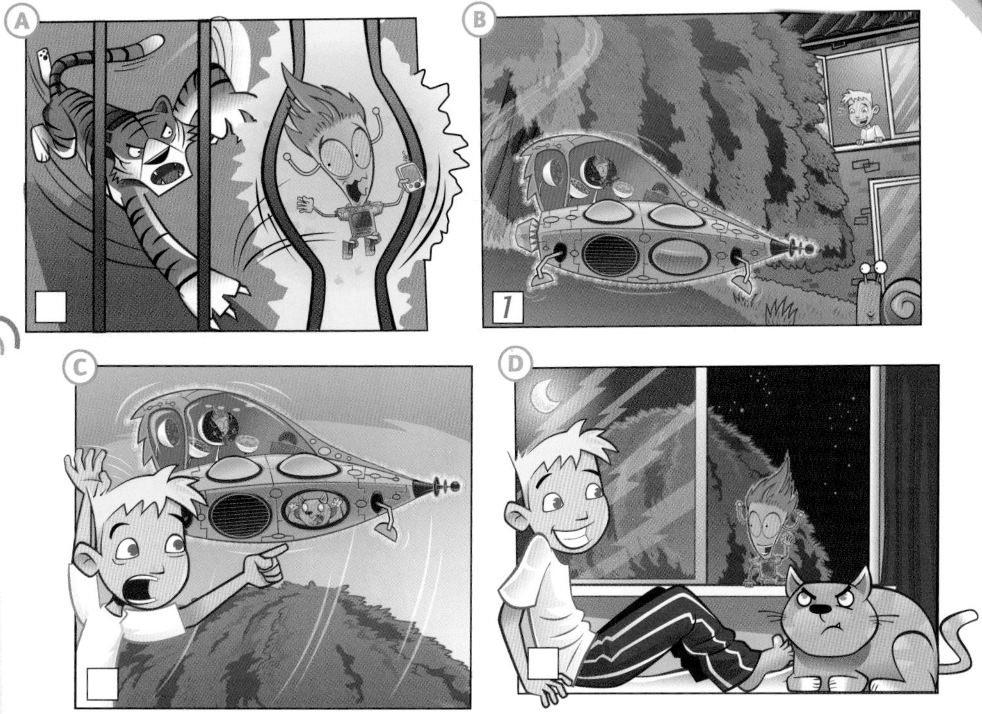

7 **Now retell the story. Use *first, then, after that, finally* and these verbs.**

came met liked hated went saw

Fun Zone

8 3.42 **Listen and complete. Listen again and rap.**

Zappedy Zap!
One Two Three
They [1] *came* to Earth
What did they [2] ____?
A thing called [3] ____
Ugly and fat
A boy [4] ____ Kit
And a good-looking cat

They [5] ____ scary zappers
Big red toes
Short blue hair
And a purple nose
The people were scared on [6] ____
The aliens went [7] ____
because of me!

DISCOVER SKILLS 9d

Star Report

Reading

1 3.43 Order the sentences. Read, listen and check.

a Natalie was in *Star Wars*.
b She went to theatre camp.
c She studied different languages.
d Natalie moved to America. *1*
e She was in the film *Leon*.

Natalie Portman in *Star Wars*

Star REPORT

Natalie Portman is a big star in Hollywood today. What do we know about her?

Well, her real name is Natalie Hershlag. Her family moved to America when Natalie was three.

Natalie went to school in New York. She had dance classes after school and in the holidays she went to theatre camp. She was good in all the plays at camp.

Her first film was called *Leon*. She was very young – only thirteen years old! She was a child star but she didn't work on films every day. She went to school too. Then, when she finished school, she went to university. She studied different languages.

After that, she was in lots of films. Do you remember her in *Star Wars*? She was Padme Amidala in three of the films. She was fantastic!

2 Read and answer the questions.

1 Where did she go to school? *New York*
2 When did she have dance classes?
3 What did she do in the holidays?
4 Was she a child star?
5 What are the names of her films?

Try this!

To remember English words:

- translate the word.
- write it in a sentence.
- draw the word.

Listening

3 🎧 **3.44 Listen. Which city did Marty go to?**

4 🎧 **3.45 Listen again and complete the sentences.**

1 Marty went to New York with his *mum and dad*.
2 The Empire State Building was in the film ________________.
3 Marty's ________________ didn't like the musical *Chicago*.
4 They didn't go on a ________________ because it was cold .
5 They didn't meet ________________.

Speaking

5 **Imagine a visit to a city. Work with a friend. Ask and answer.**

1 Where did you go last week? Paris / London / Milan
2 What did you see? A musical / A film / A concert / An exhibition
3 Did you like it? Yes / No / It was boring / fantastic / exciting / terrible
4 Did you see any famous people? Christina Aguilera / Daniel Radcliffe / Kiera Knightly

Writing

6 **Write a Star Report for your favourite film star.**

- What is his / her name?
- Where is he / she from?
- Was he / she a child star?
- What are the names of his / her films?
- What was your favourite film?

9e Let's Revise!

Words

1 Find six adjectives in the wordsearch.

t	e	r	r	i	b	l	e	w	e
s	c	t	r	a	i	p	x	m	t
j	o	f	r	p	w	b	c	n	i
f	a	n	t	a	s	t	i	c	e
u	r	f	u	t	r	p	t	l	d
n	d	t	b	o	f	u	i	t	s
n	e	t	e	r	g	i	n	o	c
y	s	s	r	l	a	z	g	j	a
t	a	b	o	r	i	n	g	g	r
y	f	u	t	y	f	n	l	s	y

2 Complete the sentences.

concerts musical ~~TV programmes~~ play films exhibition

1 We watch *__TV programmes__* on TV.
2 Summer pop ___________ are in the park.
3 There is an art ___________ at school today.
4 There are some famous actors in the ___________.
5 A ___________ has song and dance.
6 We watch ___________ at the cinema.

Grammar

3 Complete the sentences. Use the past simple.

1 Yesterday I *__met__* (meet) Tanya at the park.
2 My friend Jo ______ (come) too.
3 After the park we ______ (go) to Tanya's house.
4 I ______ (take) an old DVD of *Star Wars*.
5 The film ______ (have) Natalie Portman in it.
6 We ______ (see) the start of the film, but it was boring.

4 Order the questions. Write the answers.

1 you last month Did go to the cinema ?
Did you go to the cinema last month?
2 did What film you see ?
3 any good songs Did have it ?
4 Did meet your friends you ?
5 take Did any sweets you ?
6 go did Where you after the film ?

Pronunciation /ʊ/ /uː/

5 3.46 Listen and repeat.

Have a good look at your cool school book.

Functions

6 Order the sentences and write two stories.

1 Finally she was with all her friends.
2 Then there were two.
3 First she saw Megan and Finn. *1B*
4 Finally Alex had the last ice cream.
5 After that she saw Mary too.
6 First there were three ice creams. *1A*

A

B

Checklist

I can talk about entertainment.
I can use irregular past tenses.
I can give my opinion.
I can use sequencers.
I can order events.

10 Adventure

Hi!
This month's webpage is about adventures. Look at our photos!

Discover Words

places and activities

1 3.47 Listen, repeat and find these in the photos.

mountain *4, 5* river lake forest camping hiking canoeing rock climbing mountain-biking

2 3.48 Listen and match the photos.

1 =
2 =

3 Describe a photo. Your friends guess.

A *There are trees, mountain bikes and a river.*
B *Photo 1!*

IN THIS UNIT:

- places and activities
- revision of tenses
- camping equipment
- *want to*
- expressing preferences

Discover 5 extra words. Go to page 109.

10a Young Explorers

www.DiscoveryWeb/explorers

Hi, everyone! It's the summer holidays and time for adventure! Email your stories, but first read about Kate.

Hi! My name is Kate. I'm twelve years old and I'm sailing around the world with my family. My little brother Nat and I don't go to school. We have lessons with our mum and dad on the boat. Geography is our favourite subject because we often visit the places in our books.

We started our adventure in California, then we went to Mexico. Now we're in Australia. Our granny lives here. She's 60 years old and she can surf! This morning was exciting because we saw a shark. It was scary but we were lucky – it didn't see us.

Sailing is fun! I like swimming and I love sailing the boat with dad. I can cook too, but Nat can't – he's lazy! I don't like bad weather. When it rains it's boring. We haven't got a TV so I read or listen to music. At the moment it isn't raining. It's sunny and hot. We're all on the beach and we're having fish for lunch!

1 3.49 **Listen, read and complete the table.**

Kate's adventure	
with	1 her parents, *her brother*
in	2 California, ________
likes	3 ________
doesn't like	4 ________

2 Read and answer the questions.

1 Do Kate and Nat go to school? *No, they don't.*
2 What is Kate's favourite subject?
3 What can Kate's granny do?
4 Have they got a TV?
5 What's the weather like at the moment?
6 What are they doing now?

Grammar revision of tenses

present simple
We **have lessons** with our parents.

present continuous
I'**m sailing** around the world.

past simple
We **started** in California.

3 Look at the webpage. Find two sentences, one positive and one negative, for each tense.

4 Complete the sentences with a verb in the correct tense.

1 We *went* (go) to Sydney yesterday.
2 Granny ________ (have got) a flat in Sydney.
3 It rained, so we ________ (not go) to the beach.
4 I ________ (take) lots of photos.
5 Today we ________ (write) e-mails at an Internet café.
6 Granny often ________ (come) here.
7 Granny ________ (talk) to Nat now.
8 Nat ________(not listen). He's eating an ice cream.

Watch Out!

climb *climbed*
go *went*

Listening

5 3.50 Listen to another adventure. Answer the questions.

1 Where is Mark?
2 What type of holiday is it?

6 3.51 Listen again. Circle the correct words.

1 Mark is on holiday with his family / his friends.
2 They are staying in a hotel / a tent.
3 They are near a lake / a forest.
4 Mark cycled 30 km / 13 km this morning.
5 His sister is bored / tired.
6 Mark usually goes swimming / goes sailing in the afternoon.
7 He likes eating pizza / ice cream.

7 Read and choose.

1 This summer we're on holiday in ...

2 We're staying in a ...

3 Yesterday it was ...

4 We went to a lake by ...

5 We saw a ...

Writing

8 Now write about your adventure.

This summer we're on holiday in the mountains ...

10b Camping

Discover Words

camping

1 3.52 **Match the words with the objects in the photo. Listen and repeat.**

map *5* sleeping bag torch rucksack compass rope hiking boots

2 3.53 **Listen and read. True or false?**

1 The children are at school. *false*
2 Felix and Monica went rock climbing.
3 Gemma doesn't like canoeing.
4 Felix never goes hiking.
5 There's an elephant in Gemma's rucksack.
6 She can't stand up with her rucksack.

The children are at Summer Camp.

Ben Hey, Felix! What did you do this morning?
Felix We went rock climbing. I go everyday.
Monica It was scary, but great fun.
Gemma Ben and I went canoeing. I didn't really like it. It was a nightmare!
Monica Oh Ben! There's a hike this afternoon. Do you want to go?
Ben No, thanks.
Felix But it's fun! We always go hiking at Summer Camp.
Ben But I'm tired.
Monica What's Gemma doing?
Felix She's looking for her rucksack. Can you see it in the tent?
Monica No, I can't. What a mess!
Ben It's here, Gemma. Wow! Have you got an elephant in that bag?
Gemma No! but there's a rope, my compass and a torch.
Ben But you can't stand up with that rucksack!
Gemma Watch me! Aaargh!
Felix/Ben/Monica Oh Gemma!

Talking Tips!

3 3.54 **Listen, repeat and match.**

1 It's a nightmare!
2 What a mess!

(A)

(B)

Grammar revision of tenses

What did you do this morning? We went rock climbing.	**past simple**
Do you go hiking every day? Yes, I do.	**present simple**
What's Gemma doing? She's looking for her rucksack.	**present continuous**

4 Order the questions, then add these words.

yesterday at the moment everyday

1 you go swimming Do ?
2 you the mountains Did go to ?
3 wearing you hiking boots Are ?

5 Practise Exercise 4 with a friend. Change the words in purple.

Do you go mountain biking every day?

Why is the Mississippi a strange river?
Because it's got four eyes but can't see!

Fun Zone

6 Read and complete.

At the moment Fred and Fenella Forest are camping. They always go camping in the summer. Their 1  *tent* is in a forest near a 2  ________. Fred loves camping! He's got a new 3  ________ and new 4  ________. Yesterday it was sunny. Fred went climbing in the 5  ________, but Fenella didn't go. Fenella never goes climbing and she can't cook. At the moment it is raining. Fenella is hungry and she's talking on her mobile phone. 'Hi! A big pizza please. We're camping in a 6 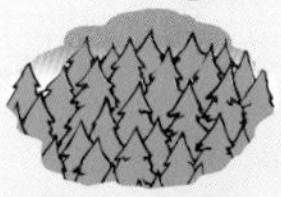 ________ near a river. Oh no! Where's my 7 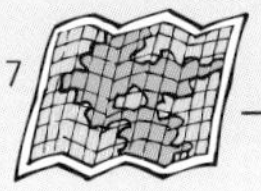 ________?'

7 Complete the questions. Use the present simple, present continuous and past simple.

1 Fred and Fenella / on holiday / at the moment?
Are Fred and Fenella on holiday at the moment?
2 they / always / go camping / in the summer?
3 Fenella / got a new rucksack?
4 what / Fred / do yesterday?
5 Fenella / often / go climbing?
6 who / Fenella / talking to / at the moment?

10c Earth Explorer

1 3.55 **Listen and read.**

2 **True or false?**

1 Fiz is going home. *true*
2 Kit can go to Fiz's planet.
3 Kit has got a present from Fiz.
4 Bandit is in the house.
5 He's feeling tired.
6 Bandit likes flying.

3 **Act out the Earth Explorer cartoon with your friends.**

Grammar *want to*

I You We They	**want to** **don't want to**	get out.
He She It	**wants to** **doesn't want to**	

Do you **want to** come with me?
Yes, I do. / No, I don't.

Functions: expressing preferences

4 **Look at the list. Tick the things you want to do.**

- climb a mountain ☐
- sail to Australia ☐
- go to another planet ☐
- be a film star ☐
- live in a forest ☐

5 **Work with a friend. Ask and answer.**

A *Do you want to climb a mountain?*
B *Yes, I do. / No, I don't.*

6 **Now write about your friend.**

Alice doesn't want to climb a mountain. She wants to sail to Australia.

Fun Zone

7 3.56 **Complete the song. Use these words.**

fly alone ~~home~~ goodbye dad bad

I want to see my planet, Kit.
I want to see my [1] *home*,
I want to go in my spaceship
But I don't want to go [2] ____.

Do you want to come to my planet, Kit?
Do you want to meet my [3] ____?
Do you want to fly in space with me?
My spaceship isn't [4] ____.

I want to come in your spaceship, Fiz.
I really want to [5] ____.
But Mum wants me here with her,
So it's time to say [6] ____.

8 3.57 **Listen again. Check and sing.**

9 **Help Bandit with his report. Find the sentences.**

REPORT FROM SPACE

It's|hot|here!Idon'tlikeeatingbats' legs,butIlovespaceboards!

It's hot …

10d Let's Revise!

Words

1 Circle the odd one out.

1 map (river) compass torch
2 forest mountain hiking boots lake
3 canoeing hiking mountain biking rope
4 tent sleeping bag rucksack mountain

2 Find the words from Exercise 1 in the photo.

Grammar

3 Complete Gemma's letter. Use the present simple, present continuous or the past simple.

Hi Mum

I [1] *'m having* (have) a nice time at Summer Camp. I always do! Yesterday I [2] ____ (go) hiking with Monica. At first it was sunny, but then it rained – it [3] ____ (not stop) all morning! In the end we [4] ____ (hurry) back to camp.

I [5] ____ (always / get up) early here. Felix doesn't – he's lazy! At the moment I'm in my tent and I [6] ____ (listen) to some music. I've got Granddad's torch but it's old so I [7] _______ (not often use) it. Summer Camp is great – and it [8] ____ (not rain) now. Hurray!

Love Gemma xx

4 Complete the questions. Answer them.

1 *Does* Gemma always *have* (have) a nice time at Summer Camp?
2 What _____ she _____ (do) with Monica yesterday?
3 What _____ (be) the weather like in the morning?
4 _____ Felix usually_____ (get up) early?
5 What _____ Gemma _____ (listen) to at the moment?
6 _____ she often_______ (use) granddad's torch?

Pronunciation /ɪ/ /aɪ/

5 3.58 Listen and repeat.

Fiz is riding a bike by a nice big river.

Functions

6 Look at the Summer Camp activities. Complete the sentences.

	Gemma	Monica	Felix	Ben
rock climbing	✗	✓	✓	✗
mountain-biking	✓	✓	✓	✓
canoeing	✗	✗	✓	✗
hiking	✓	✓	✗	✗

1 Gemma *doesn't want to* go rock climbing.
2 Monica ___________ go hiking.
3 Ben ___________ go canoeing.
4 Felix ___________ go rock climbing.
5 All the children ___________ go mountain-biking.

7 Imagine you are at Summer Camp. Ask and answer.

A *Do you want to go rock climbing?*
B *Yes, I do. / No, I don't.*

Consolidation

8 3.59 Listen and complete the dialogue.

Felix Hi, Ben. What [1] *are* you doing?
Ben Nothing ... I'm [2] ______ !
Felix Do you [3] ______ go to the cinema today?
Ben I [4] ______ yesterday with my sister. We [5] ______ every Thursday.
Felix Oh right! What did you [6] ______?
Ben The new *Pirates of the Caribbean*.
Felix Was it [7] ______?
Ben No, it was [8] ______ . Jack's magic [9] ______ is ...
Felix Shshshsh!! I don't [10] ______ know! I want to see it!
Ben But you [11] ______ me!

9 Now practise the dialogue with a friend.

Checklist ✓

- I can describe places and activities. ☐
- I can use different tenses. ☐
- I can talk about camping. ☐
- I can say what I want to do. ☐

Song

10 3.60 Listen and complete the song. Use these words.

watch ~~see~~ photographs ocean rain see

You Belong to Me

[1] *See* the pyramids around the Nile
[2] ______ the sunrise from a tropic isle
Just remember darling all the while
You belong to me.

See the marketplace in old Algiers
Send me [3] ______ and souvenirs
Just remember when a dream appears.
You belong to me

And I'll be so alone without you
Maybe you'll be lonesome too

Fly the [4] ______ in a silver plane
See the jungle when it's wet with [5] ______

Just remember till you're home again
You belong to me

11 3.61 Now listen and sing.

10e Discover Culture

Captain Cook came from England. He was a great explorer and travelled to New Zealand and Australia.

Today people can go from Europe to New Zealand in twenty-four hours, but in the past, the voyage was long and dangerous. In 1769 James Cook sailed around New Zealand. Then he went to Australia. He met the Aborigines there and discovered the kangaroo. After that he went to the Antarctic and to the Pacific islands. He was the first European in lots of these places.

We know about Captain Cook's adventures from his diaries and his maps. Other people used Cook's maps and went to Australia and New Zealand after him. Today the Australians and New Zealanders all speak English.

Reading

1 3.62 **Read, listen and order the places Captain Cook visited.**

a Antarctica
b New Zealand *1*
c Pacific islands
d Australia

2 Read and complete the sentences.

1 Captain Cook came from ***England***.
2 In 1769, he met the ____________.
3 In Australia, he discovered ____________.
4 Today people in Australia and ____________ speak ____________.

Project

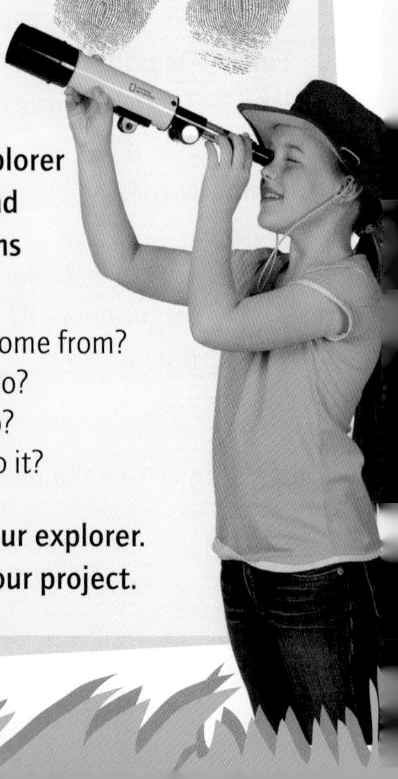

Explorers

3 Think of an explorer from history. Ask and answer the questions with a friend.

1 Where did they come from?
2 Where did they go?
3 What did they do?
4 When did they do it?

4 Write about your explorer. Find a picture for your project.

Find extra words!

Go to these pages and find these words in the pictures or photos.

UNIT 1 page 10	UNIT 3 page 30	UNIT 5 page 52	UNIT 7 page 74	UNIT 9 pages 90-91
beach ball	bee	candle	cobwebs	actor
dunes	elephant	cushion	costumes	actress
flip-flops	kangaroo	plant	haunted house	audience
sand	koala	rug	mask	curtains
sky	zebra	TV remote control	pumpkin	stage

UNIT 2 page 19	UNIT 4 page 40	UNIT 6 page 59	UNIT 8 page 79	UNIT 10 page 99
armchair	butter	diving board	blackboard	canoe
cooker	marmalade	post box	computers	cliff
lamp	milk	shopping trolley	globe	helmet
wardrobe	orange juice	traffic lights	musical instruments	lake
washing machine	toast	zebra crossing	paint brush	tent

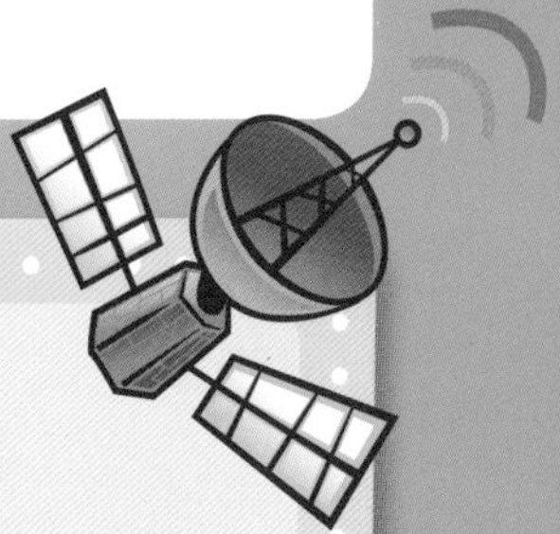

CODE BREAKER

Word list

STARTER

countries
Argentina
Brazil
England
Greece
Italy
Poland
Portugal
Russia
Spain
Turkey
USA

nationalities
American
Argentinian
Brazilian
English
Greek
Italian
Polish
Portuguese
Russian
Spanish
Turkish

favourite things
animal
baseball cap
camera
CD player
football shirt
mobile phone
MP3 player
skateboard
watch

subject pronouns
I
you
he
she
it
we
they

possessive pronouns
my
your
his
her
its
our
their

colours
black
purple
red
yellow

numbers
five
six
ten
eleven

other
age
am
and
are / aren't
but
cat
city
class
Discovery Web
dog
earth
explorer
family
friend
from
hello
hey
hi
home
how old?
in
is / isn't
mouse
new
no
not
outer space
spaceship
team
that
the
these
this
those
too
website
what?
who?
year

UNIT 1

appearance adjectives
fat
good-looking
old
short
tall
thin
ugly
young

the family
mum
dad
brother
sister
aunt
uncle
cousin
granny
granddad

things for the beach
beach bag
drink
frisbee
ice cream
towel

other
about
blonde
body
book
boy
car
chocolate
cool
email
er ...
factory
famous
far away
film
for
funny
game
girl
gold
great
green
ha! ha!
hair
has got
have got
here
look (at)
man
meet
member
miaow
name
now
oh no!
or
orange
page
people
photo
professor
sandwich
school
star (= famous person)
team
thanks
town
toy
try
wait
wait and see
welcome (to)
well, ...
where?
which?
with
yes
zapper

UNIT 2

rooms
attic
bathroom
bedroom
garden
kitchen
living room
stairs

prepositions of place
behind
in
next to
on
under

furniture
bath
bed
bookcase
chair
cupboard
desk
fridge
mirror
shower
sofa
table
toilet

instructions
be quick
don't touch
hurry up
listen

open the door
sit down
stay there

other
any
at
big
bike
castle
cat
choose
come and see
cooker
crash
dark
door
flat
food
fun
ghost
ghoul
helmet
help
hot
house
idea
joke
king
letter
light
lots of
May
message
nice
oh yeah
OK
only
plane
please
purple
right
secret
so
some
someone
spooky
television
there
today

treehouse
truth
TV
typical
underground
understand
well
window
wow!

UNIT 3

animals
bat
chameleon
dolphin
elephant
giraffe
monkey
parrot
shark
squirrel
tiger
turtle

action verbs
climb
dance
fly
jump
paint
play music
run
sing
swim
water ski
body parts
arm
ear
eye
finger
foot / feet
hair
hand
head
leg
mouth
neck
nose
tooth/teeth

adjectives
beautiful
clever
dangerous
fast
slow

other
aarrggh!
act
amazing
Asia
Australia
bad luck
banana
because
come on
cry
dear
eat
exhibition
guide
key
let's go
move
no way!
of course
orchestra
ouch!
pet
picture
place
play the drums
play the guitar
postcard
roar!
robot
rock (v)
Sandtiger shark
say
shhh!
song
soon
soul
stand
take
talk
Thai
think
touch

walk
wave
woof!
write
zoo

UNIT 4

routine verbs
finish school
get up
go to bed
have dinner
meet friends
study
walk to school
watch TV

transport
bike
boat
bus
car
motorbike
plane
train
the time
five to twelve
half past eight
quarter past three
seven o'clock
ten to nine
twenty-five to six

food and meals
breakfast
lunch
dinner
apple
fish and chips
pizza
sandwiches
sweets
toast

other
bee
before
brrr
buzz
by
cereal

cold
crisscross
disgusting
do
does
doesn't
don't
every
flying
go away
goal
goodnight
homework
hop
hour
India
knee
lake
late
left
live
ow!
read
same
show
skate park
slide
spaceboard
stomp
tell the time
vampire
visit
what time is it?
when
yummy

UNIT 5

sports with *play*
basketball
football
golf
tennis
volleyball

sports with *go*
cycling
horse riding
sailing
swimming
windsurfing

the seasons
spring
summer
autumn
winter

times of day
morning
afternoon
evening
night

object pronouns
me
you
him
her
it
us
them
other
activity
ask
camp
crazy
hate
hero
how about …?
kitesurfing
like
love
match
near
other
stadium
stop
teacher
train (v)
use
water
weekend
world champion

UNIT 6

places in town
bus station
café
cinema
library
park
police station
post office
supermarket
swimming pool

clothes
boots
coat
dress
hat
jeans
jumper
shoes
shorts
skirt
socks
trousers
T-shirt

directions
go past
go straight on
on the left
on the right
turn left
turn right

other
angry
at the moment
autograph
bad
bubble
called
clue
competition
detective
different
don't be silly
excuse me
feel
film studio
follow
gadget
go shopping
happy
How embarrassing!
language
magazine
magnifying glass
money
museum
mystery
police
post a letter
puzzle
scared
sir
smile
spy
story
sunglasses
the news
thief
tree
trip
wait a minute!
wear
well done
winner
You're joking!

UNIT 7

the months
January
February
March
April
May
June
July
August
September
October
November
December

frequency adverbs
always
usually
often
sometimes
never

ordinal numbers
first
second
third
fourth
fifth
sixth
seventh
eighth
ninth
tenth
eleventh
twelfth

the weather
cloudy
cold
foggy
hot
rain
snow
sunny
windy

other
again
all
band
basket
birthday
bucket
buy
cake
card
carnival
celebrate
celebration
Chinese
Christmas
cook (v)
date
diary
dragon
Easter
egg
fantastic
festival
firework
game
Hallowe'en
Holi
New Year
nobody
party
play tricks
present
queen
rock
scary
special
street
That's not fair!
throw
tradition
trick-or-treating
work (v)
yippee

UNIT 8

school subjects
art
computer studies
English
French
geography
history
maths
music
P.E.
science

feelings
angry
bored
hungry
sad
scared
thirsty
tired
worried

other
band practice
break
careful
comment
crash (v)
disappear
don't worry
experiment (n)
last
lesson
lucky
Move over!
nothing
painter
prince
project
real